NUTRITION
and FOOD HYGIENE

Philippa Hudson ◆ *Catherine Symonds*

Hodder & Stoughton

A MEMBER OF THE HODDER HEADLINE GROUP

Orders: please contact Bookpoint Ltd, 39 Milton Park, Abingdon, Oxon OX14 4TD.
Telephone: (44) 01235 400414, Fax: (44) 01235 400454. Lines are open from 9.00 - 6.00, Monday to Saturday, with a 24 hour message answering service. Email address: orders@bookpoint.co.uk

British Library Cataloguing in Publication Data

Hudson, Philippa
  Nutrition and food hygiene
  1. Nutrition   2. Food handling   3. Food service
  I. Title   II. Symonds, Catherine
  641.1

ISBN 0 340 643 463

First published 1996

Impression number	12	11	10	9	8	7	6	5	4	3	
Year		2005	2004	2003	2002	2001	2000	1999			

Typeset byFakenham Photosetting Limited, Fakenham, Norfolk.
Printed in Great Britain for Hodder & Stoughton Educational, a division of Hodder Headline Plc, 338 Euston Road, London NW1 3BH by Scotprint Ltd, Musselburgh, Scotland.

Contents

Introduction
What is this book about?

The choice of foods available today is extremely wide compared to a few years ago. An increasing amount of food is eaten outside the home. The public has a right to expect food to be of good quality. They do not expect it to make them ill, e.g. by food poisoning. In recent years there has also been more interest in the effect that food has on our health; however, food must still look and taste good. The aim of this book is to introduce catering students to the subjects of food and health, and food hygiene. It will also be of use to students on other types of course that include food preparation.

A good place to start is the question, 'What is food'? Simply, food is any substance of plant or animal origin that when eaten and absorbed by the body produces energy, promotes the growth and repair of body tissues, or regulates the body processes. The components of food that perform these effects are called nutrients. Nutrition is the study of food (or nutrients) and the effect it has on the body. It includes the factors that affect food intake.

But food does not just contain nutrients. It contains water which is also essential to life, and various substances that give food colour and flavour. There are other substances that might be put into food such as additives or may just get into food accidentally such as pesticide residues. Many foods also contain a whole range of micro-organisms. The presence of these organisms may be beneficial or they may cause food spoilage or food poisoning.

Micro-organisms can be deliberately added to food during production, e.g. bread, wine and cheese, or the micro-organisms already present can spoil the food. As spoilage is ultimately inevitable, a whole range of preservation techniques have been developed to try to increase the shelf-life (or keeping quality) of our food. Some micro-organisms contaminate our food and cause illness rather than spoilage. Every effort must be made to keep our food free from these micro-organisms. To fully understand the mechanisms by which the processes of spoilage and contamination can be controlled, you need to understand the basics of food microbiology and hygiene. This book introduces you to basic food microbiology and then shows you how to prevent food spoilage and food poisoning by applying this information to catering.

Caterers and other people involved in food production have a moral and legal responsibility to ensure that food is safe. Food should also be nutritious, but this does not mean that cream cakes should be automatically banned in favour of lettuce and cucumber. Healthy eating is about consuming the correct amount of nutrients for the needs of the individual, and hence contributing to the health of that individual. There are no good or bad foods, only good or bad diets. As caterers you need to be able to provide a wide range of different types of meals depending on the type of establishment you are working in. You will increasingly have to provide your customers with information about the meals you serve so that they can choose whether they wish to eat a low fat meal, for example. It is not about making people eat certain foods but providing a range of meals along with the advice and information so that the customer can choose.

This book will help you to provide safe nutritious meals for your customers. It will be useful if you are studying NVQ, GNVQ, BTEC, National Diploma or the first year of BTEC Higher National Diploma and degree programmes in food related areas.

Exercises

Within each chapter of this book you will find exercises and self-check questions which support the particular subject area. Some of these are written exercises, while others are more practical. Within the hygiene section you will find some suggestions of laboratory based practicals which could be used to complement the information in the text. Whilst every care has been taken to ensure that these practicals provide the necessary information, the following precautions must be taken:

◆ only carry out practical microbiology in an appropriate laboratory
◆ ensure that a thorough COSHH assessment of all the practical exercises is carried out in-house before they are used
◆ ensure that appropriate protective clothing is available
◆ ensure that appropriate disposal procedures are available: either incinerate or autoclave ALL hazardous and potentially hazardous waste.

1

Basics of Human Nutrition

This chapter examines all the nutrients that we must obtain from food, the types of foods that we get them from and the effect of cooking or processing on nutrients. Although water is not a nutrient, it is essential for life and so water is also included in this section. How our body obtains the nutrients from the food we eat is essential for an understanding of nutrition. The last section introduces you to the concept of food energy or Calories as it is more widely known.

CARBOHYDRATES

By the end of this section you should be able to
- distinguish between mono, di and polysaccharides
- give examples of these types of carbohydrates
- understand the difference between intrinsic and extrinsic sugars
- explain what is meant by the term 'non-starch polysaccharides'

Introduction

Carbohydrates are an important group of nutrients in the diet; their main function is providing energy. Their structures are all based on a common unit called a **saccharide** unit. This unit is nearly always glucose, and the grouping or classification of carbohydrates depends primarily on the number of saccharide units each carbohydrate contains. This can vary from one to many thousands.

Sugars	MONOSACCHARIDES	one unit (mono meaning one)
	DISACCHARIDES	two units (di meaning two)
Non-sugars	POLYSACCHARIDES	many units (poly meaning many)

Monosaccharides (simple sugars)

Three types of sugar are important:

1   **Glucose** (sometimes called dextrose) is the most important monosaccharide. It occurs naturally in fruit and plant juices, and in the

blood of living animals. Most carbohydrates in food are ultimately converted to glucose during digestion.

2   **Fructose** occurs naturally in some fruit and vegetables and especially in honey. It is the sweetest sugar known and is often called fruit sugar.

3   **Galactose** does not exist as such in foods but is produced when lactose (a disaccharide) is broken down during digestion (see below).

Disaccharides

Disaccharides consist of two monosaccharides linked together:

1   **Sucrose** occurs naturally in sugar cane and sugar beet and in some roots (e.g. carrots) and fruits. Table sugar, as sucrose is often called, is a chemical combination of glucose and fructose.

2   **Maltose** is formed during the breakdown of starch by digestion and during the germination or sprouting of barley (important in beer production). It is a combination of two glucose units.

3   **Lactose** occurs only in milk, including human milk. It is less sweet than sucrose or glucose and is a combination of glucose and galactose.

Sugars are also grouped on the basis of where they occur in foods (i.e. *inside* or *outside* the cell walls of foods).

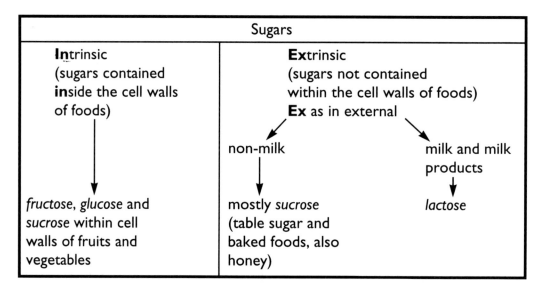

Table 1: Classification of sugars

We are being encouraged to eat more fruit and vegetables, hence our intake of intrinsic sugars should rise. However, our intake of the extrinsic sugar sucrose is already extremely high and so most authorities recommend a reduction in this type of sugar.

Properties of sugars (Monosaccharides & Disaccharides)

1   All sugars are white crystalline compounds which are soluble in water (i.e. they dissolve in water).

2   All sugars are sweet but they do not have the same degree of sweetness.

3   When sugars are heated they caramelise.

4   Sugars can act as preservatives if large amounts are present in a food, e.g. jam.

Polysaccharides

These are formed from a varying number of monosaccharide units. They are usually insoluble in cold water (i.e. do not dissolve in cold water) and are tasteless.

Polysaccharides in food fall into three groups:

1   **Starch** is the most important polysaccharide. It is the major food reserve of plants and is a mixture of two polysaccharides called **amylose** and **amylopectin**.

    Starch is a white powder and does not have a sweet taste. If you heat a mixture of starch in water it eventually thickens; this is the reason why sauces thicken when you heat them. On heating, the starch granules swell and eventually gelatinise.

2   **Glycogen** is a carbohydrate found only in animals, where small amounts are stored in the liver and muscles, and act as an energy reserve. Glycogen is composed of branched chains of glucose units, but unlike amylopectin it is soluble in water. We do not eat very much glycogen because it breaks down again to glucose after the animal is slaughtered.

3   **Non-Starch Polysaccharides** (**NSP**) (or **dietary fibre**) provide the rigid and fibrous structure of vegetables, fruits and cereal grains. They form the main part of food that is not digested. The term 'dietary fibre' was widely

used to describe this part of food. However, the amount of fibre found in foods appeared to vary depending on which method of chemical analysis had been used. Therefore, to obtain some standardisation, a specific method of chemical analysis has been agreed upon. This measures the amount of non-starch polysaccharide (NSP) in a food (i.e. the amount of polysaccharide other than starch). The term NSP may replace dietary fibre in future.

NSP is made up of the following:

<u>a</u>   *Cellulose* consists of many thousands of glucose units. It cannot be digested by man because we do not have the necessary enzymes to break it down. Cellulose is important for providing roughage or bulk in the diet and therefore assisting in the passage of digestible materials and waste products through the intestines.

<u>b</u>   *Pectin* and other similar polysaccharides are found in many fruits and some root vegetables, e.g. turnips. Apples and the peel of citrus fruits are particularly rich in pectin. Its main importance is as a gelling agent, e.g. in jam making.

<u>c</u>   *Hemicelluloses* and other polysaccharides are found in small amounts.

The old term 'dietary fibre' included all the above plus other non-digestible plant material such as the woody material lignin.

Functions of carbohydrates in the diet

After eating foods containing polysaccharides and disaccharides, they are hydrolysed (broken down) by digestive enzymes. All carbohydrates are absorbed as monosaccharides. As part of the digestive process the monosaccharides fructose and galactose are converted into glucose. Thus almost all digested carbohydrates are eventually converted to glucose.

Glucose has two main functions in the body:

1   **Energy**   Glucose is oxidised in the cells with the release of energy. This energy can be used for physical activity but more usually it is needed by body cells for normal functioning: 1g of carbohydrate provides 3.75kcal (16kJ).

2   **Converted into body fat**   Any carbohydrate you eat that you do not immediately need for energy may be converted into body fat. This conversion takes place in the liver but the fat is stored all over the body, mainly in the adipose tissue under the skin.

Sources of carbohydrate in the diet

1 **Cereals and Cereal Foods**   All cereals contain a high percentage of starch. The main cereals consumed in the UK are wheat, rice, maize (corn), oats, rye and barley. Cereal foods account for 40% of the total carbohydrate content of the average British diet.

2 **Refined Sugar (sucrose)**   Sugar is eaten in large quantities, as table sugar and in manufactured goods such as biscuits, sweets, ice cream, jams and soft drinks. Sugar and preserves account for 11% of the total carbohydrate content of the average British diet.

3 **Vegetables**   Vegetables contain starch and sugars in varying amounts. Potatoes are the richest source of carbohydrate although pulse vegetables (e.g. beans) also contain significant amounts. They account for 14% of the total carbohydrate content of the average British diet.

4 **Fruits**   As fruit ripens starch is turned into sugar. Most fruits contain between 5% and 10% sugar. Bananas are the only fruit which contain starch as well as sugar when ripe. Fruits contribute on average 7% of the total carbohydrate content.

5 **Milk**   Milk and milk products such as yoghurt contain the sugar lactose. They contribute 8% of the total carbohydrate content of the average British diet. Foods such as cheese and butter made from milk do not contain lactose because the whey part of milk which contains lactose is discarded during cheese and butter production.

Dietary guidelines

We are recommended to eat more starchy foods like cereals and also fruit and vegetables. Starches should provide 39% of our daily energy (Calorie) intake and sugars (mainly sucrose) 11%.

In addition we should aim to eat 18g/day of NSP with a range of 12–24g/day. Because of their smaller body weight children should eat less.

More information about the role of NSP is given in the next chapter.

SELF CHECK QUESTIONS

---

1   *Give three examples each of monosaccharides, disaccharides, and polysaccharides.*
2   *What is the main extrinsic sugar we eat?*
3   *What is the main function of glucose in the body?*
4   *Define the term NSP.*

LIPIDS (FATS AND OILS)

By the end of this section you should be able to
- explain the difference between saturated, monounsaturated and polyunsaturated fatty acids
- know the main functions of lipids in the diet
- state the four major food sources of lipids
- state the Dietary Reference Value for total fat and saturated fatty acids

Introduction

Fats and oils (or **lipids**) include not only 'visible fats' such as butter and margarine, cooking fats and oils and the fat on meat, but also the 'invisible fats' which occur in milk, nuts, lean meat and other foods. They are a more concentrated source of energy than carbohydrates; much of the energy reserve of animals and some seeds is stored in this form. Although 'lipids' is the correct term, the term 'fats' is often used to mean both fats and oils.

Fats and oils found in food consist mainly of mixtures of triglycerides. Each triglyceride is a combination of three **fatty acids** with a unit of glycerol (glycerine). The differences between one fat or oil and another are the result of different proportions of the various fatty acids in each.

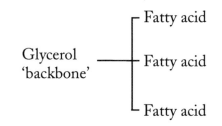

Figure 1: Triglyceride structure

Fatty acids

There are many different fatty acids found in nature. They consist of chains of carbon atoms with hydrogen atoms attached (this structure is called a hydrocarbon chain). They differ in the number of carbon atoms and double bonds which they contain. Each carbon atom can make links with a maximum of four other atoms.

Saturated fatty acids

These have no double bonds and therefore are more stable. This structure is 'saturated' with hydrogen; no more hydrogen atoms can be fitted in.

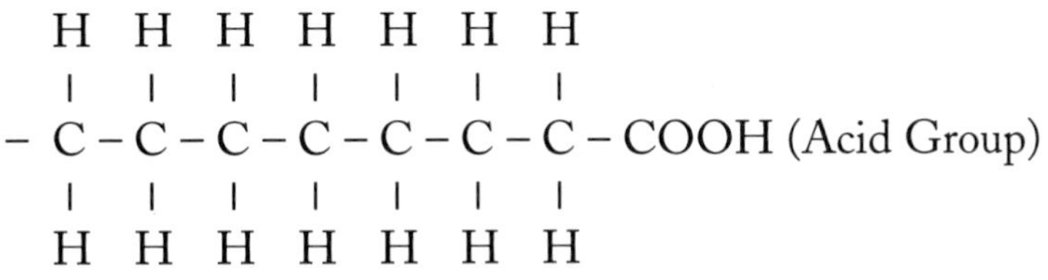

```
    H   H   H   H   H   H   H
    |   |   |   |   |   |   |
  - C - C - C - C - C - C - C - COOH (Acid Group)
    |   |   |   |   |   |   |
    H   H   H   H   H   H   H
```

Figure 2: Part of the hydrocarbon chain of a saturated fatty acid

Unsaturated fatty acids

Here the carbon chain is not saturated with hydrogen and therefore has one or more double bonds. These react gradually with air making the fat rancid.

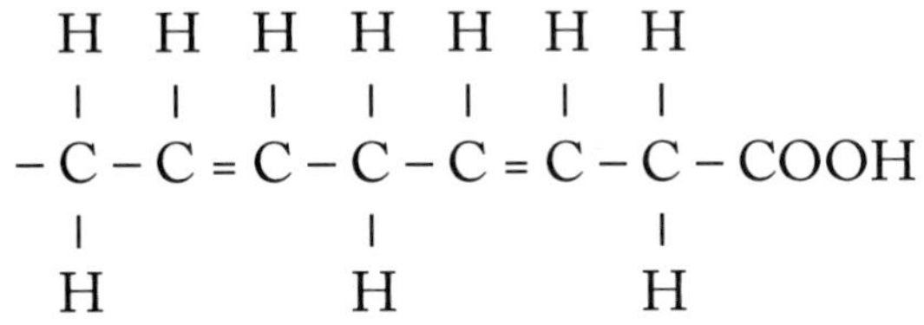

```
    H   H   H   H   H   H   H
    |   |   |   |   |   |   |
  - C - C = C - C - C = C - C - COOH
    |           |           |
    H           H           H
```

Figure 3: Part of the structure of an unsaturated fatty acid

Because each carbon atom can make links with four other atoms, it is possible to fit more hydrogen atoms into this structure by breaking the double bond; hence this structure is 'unsaturated'.

Unsaturated fatty acids may be either:

◆ Monounsaturated, containing one double bond
◆ Polyunsaturated, containing more than one double bond.

Cis and trans fatty acids

The arrangement of atoms at the double bond may vary and both mono- and polyunsaturated fatty acids can be either:

1   CIS fatty acids with the two hydrogen atoms on the same side of the double bond.

$$
\begin{array}{cc}
\text{H} & \text{H} \\
| & | \\
-\,\text{C} & = \text{C}\, -
\end{array}
$$

Naturally occurring unsaturated fatty acids are usually in the CIS configuration.

OR

2   TRANS fatty acids with the hydrogen atoms on geometrically opposite sides of the double bond.

$$
\begin{array}{c}
\text{H} \\
| \\
-\,\text{C} = \text{C}\; - \\
| \\
\text{H}
\end{array}
$$

Small amounts are found naturally in some foods but larger amounts can occur as a result of certain types of lipid processing.

There is some concern about high intakes of TRANS fatty acids and hence current recommendations are that we do not increase our intake of this type of lipid.

Properties of lipids

Fats are lipids which are solid at low temperatures and become liquid when they are heated. Oils are lipids which are liquid at room temperature, usually as a result of their higher content of unsaturated fatty acids, and will solidify on refrigeration, e.g. olive oil.

Oils and fats do not dissolve in water but may be emulsified with water by vigorous mixing as when butter and margarine are made.

Lipids make an important contribution to the texture and palatability of foods.

Furthermore, because they are digested comparatively slowly, foods rich in lipids have a high satiety value. If you eat a fatty meal you won't feel hungry as quickly as if you had eaten a high carbohydrate meal.

Food lipids usually contain small amounts of other fat soluble substances, e.g. flavour compounds and the fat soluble vitamins.

Functions of lipids in the diet

1   **Energy**   Fat is broken down in the body by oxidation and energy is released. 1g of fat provides 9kcal (37kJ). Fat has more than twice the calorific value of carbohydrates and is therefore a more concentrated source of energy.

2   **Formation of adipose tissue**   Excess fat, which is not immediately required for energy, is stored in the adipose tissue under the skin where it has three functions.

  a   an energy reserve;

  b   it forms an insulating layer and helps to prevent excessive heat loss from the body. It therefore assists in the maintenance of a constant body temperature; and

  c   when stored around delicate organs such as the kidneys, it protects these organs from physical damage.

3   **Essential fatty acids**   Some fatty acids are essential in small amounts for the functioning of the body. Linoleic acid and one form of linolenic acid (alpha – linolenic acid) are probably the only truly essential fatty acids. Linoleic acid is needed for the formation of cell membranes. Derivatives of the essential fatty acids are used to form prostaglandins, a group of hormone-like substances which help to regulate many body functions. If the diet provides 1–2% of its energy content as essential fatty acids then deficiency is unlikely. Most diets contain more than 2%.

4   **Fat soluble vitamins**   The inclusion of certain fats included in the diet help to ensure an adequate intake of the fat soluble vitamins A, D, E and K.

Sources of lipids in the diet

Fats and oils are obtained from both animals and plants.

1   **Meat and fish**   All meat contains fat, though the percentage of fat varies from animal to animal, and from one part of an animal to another. Meat provides 25% of the total fat content of the average British diet. Oily or fatty fish such as herring and mackerel contain up to 20% oil, but they contribute little fat to the British diet as they are eaten infrequently.

2   **Butter and margarine**   Butter contributes 6% and margarine a further 6% of the total fat content of the average diet.

3   **Milk, cream and cheese**   Full cream milk contains between 3% and 4% fat; some products made from milk, such as cream and cheese contain much larger amounts. Milk and milk products account for 11% of the total fat content of the average British diet, and cheese contributes a further 6%.

4   **Other foods**   Other important sources of fat are baked goods (cakes, pastries, biscuits) 8%, and vegetable oils, 8%. Many other foods contain a considerable amount of fat. These include ice cream, chocolates, some sweets, nuts and salad dressings.

Most vegetables and fruits do not contain significant amounts of fat except the soya bean (24% fat) and the avocado pear (8% fat).

Dietary guidelines

It is recommended that, on average, 35% of our energy (Calorie) intake comes from fats and oils with only 11% from saturated fatty acids. At present we eat considerably more than this and hence we are advised to eat less fat, particularly saturated fat.

SELF CHECK QUESTIONS

I   List three foods that contain significant amounts of saturated fatty acids.
2   List three foods that contain significant amounts of unsaturated fatty acids.
3   Give three reasons why we need to eat fat in our diet.

PROTEINS

By the end of this section you should be able to
- understand the basic structure of protein
- explain what is meant by the term 'essential amino acid'
- describe the main functions of protein in the body
- state the main sources of protein in the diet

Introduction

Proteins are found in all living cells of animals and plants. Protein must be provided in the diet for the growth and repair of the body, but any excess is used to provide energy. Proteins consist of chains of hundreds or even thousands of **amino acid** units. Only about 20 different amino acids are involved, but the number of ways in which they can be arranged is almost infinite. It is the unique sequence of these units which gives each protein its characteristic properties.

Of the 20 amino acids commonly found in proteins, 8 are **essential** in the diet (9 for children) and must be supplied by the foods we eat since they cannot be made in the body. The non-essential amino acids can be synthesised in the body by converting one amino acid into another within the body's cells.

Essential	Non-Essential
Isoleucine	Alanine
Leucine	Arginine
Lysine	Asparagine
Methionine	Aspartic acid
Phenylalanine	Cysteine
Threonine	Glutamic acid
Tryptophan	Glutamine
Valine	Glycine
Histidine (essential for infants)	Proline
	Serine
	Tyrosine

Table 2: Essential and non-essential amino acids

When protein foods are eaten, the proteins are hydrolysed (broken down) during digestion to produce amino acids. After absorption the amino acids are transported by the blood to the cells. In the cells the amino acids recombine and new proteins are formed.

Functions of proteins in the body

Growth and Maintenance   Proteins are the main constituents of the cells of the body. The number of cells in the body increases during periods of growth, therefore during childhood and adolescence, protein requirements are high. In addition, protein in the tissues is constantly being broken down and must be replaced from the amino acids supplied in the diet. Protein is also necessary for the formation of enzymes, antibodies and some hormones.

Energy   The diet may supply more protein than is required for growth and maintenance. Any excess protein may be used for energy: 1g of protein provides 4kcal (17kJ).

Sources of protein in the diet

Protein can be obtained from both animal and plant sources.

1   **Meat and fish**   Meat makes an important contribution to the protein content of the average British diet. Fish is eaten less frequently and hence makes a smaller contribution to protein intake.

2   **Bread and cereals**   Bread contains a significant amount of protein and is one of the most important and cheapest sources in the British diet. Other cereal foods such as rice, pasta, breakfast cereals, cakes and biscuits are also significant sources of protein.

3   **Milk and cheese**   Milk and cheese are valuable sources of good quality protein in the British diet.

4   **Eggs**   These are an excellent source of high quality protein although their contribution to the diet is small.

5   **Nuts**   Nuts are a major source of protein in the diets of many vegans and vegetarians.

Dietary guidelines

In the UK, most people eat much more protein than they need. It is recommended that we obtain 15% of our energy from protein which, for an adult, is between 45 and 55g protein per day.

---

1   Why are certain amino acids essential?

2   How many amino acids are required by
*   a) adults*
*   b) children?*

3   Give two functions of protein in the diet.

4   List three important sources of protein in the UK diet.

VITAMINS

By the end of this section you should be able to
- list the vitamins known to be important in human nutrition
- state good food sources of the individual vitamins
- describe the effect of over and under consumption of individual vitamins
- explain what effect (if any) cooking/processing has on individual vitamins

Introduction

Vitamins are substances which the body requires in small amounts, yet cannot make for itself, at least in sufficient quantities. They must, therefore, be eaten as part of the diet.

As the vitamins were discovered, each was first labelled with a letter, but once a vitamin has been isolated and its structure identified, it was given a specific name. For example, the chemical found in milk which promoted growth was given the name vitamin A.

As the vitamins were identified it became possible to divide them into two groups:-

1   Fat soluble vitamins:
       Vitamin A – retinol
       Vitamin D – cholecalciferol
       Vitamin E – tocopherol
       Vitamin K – phylloquinone

2   Water soluble vitamins:
Vitamin B_1 – thiamin
Vitamin B_2 – riboflavin
Nicotinic acid
Vitamin B_6 – pyridoxine
Vitamin B_{12} – cyanocobalamin
Folic acid
Pantothenic acid
Biotin
Vitamin C – ascorbic acid

Fat soluble vitamins can be stored in the human body, water soluble vitamins cannot. This means that an adequate daily intake of water soluble vitamins such as vitamin C is particularly important. One drawback to the body's ability to store fat soluble vitamins is that toxic levels can accumulate in the body, although this condition is rare. In general, any excess of the water soluble vitamins is immediately excreted in the urine.

Functions of vitamins

- ◆ promote health and help prevent disease
- ◆ regulate the building and repair of body cells
- ◆ help regulate the chemical reactions which release energy in body cells.

A well balanced diet will contain all the vitamins in the recommended quantities but as some foods are very poor sources of certain vitamins it is essential to choose appropriate foods.

It is rare for people in the developed countries to suffer a severe deficiency of vitamins. Some people may suffer minor deficiencies with symptoms such as tiredness, broken nails, poor condition of skin, hair and teeth. These symptoms may be due to a shortage of one or of several vitamins. The amount of each vitamin needed to promote health is more than the amount needed to prevent disease.

Fat soluble vitamins

Information about the various vitamins is given below. More detailed information is included about vitamins D and E.

	Main Functions	Rich Sources	Effect of Cooking Processes
Vitamin A (Retinols, carotenoids)	Growth, normal and night vision, protects surface tissues. Deficiency rare in the UK but the commonest cause of blindness in the third world	Liver, fish liver oils, dairy produce, eggs, carrots, green and yellow vegetables, margarine	Losses only at high temperatures, e.g. frying
Vitamin D (Cholecalciferol D_3, Ergocalciferol D_2)	Absorption and laying down of calcium and phosphorus. Deficiency causes rickets in children, osteomalacia in adults	Sunlight, fish liver oils, fatty fish, eggs, liver, margarine	Minimal
Vitamin E (α–tocopherols)	Thought to be involved in keeping cell membranes healthy by preventing oxidation of fatty substances. May be important in prevention of cancer. In foods delays the development of rancidity	Widespread but especially vegetable oils, wheatgerm, some margarines, eggs	Usually unaffected but prolonged frying can destroy Vitamin E
Vitamin K (Phylloquinone)	Blood coagulation	Leafy green vegetables, beef liver	Minimal

Table 3: Fat Soluble vitamins

Vitamin D (cholecalciferol, ergocalciferol)

Sources

The body obtains vitamin D from two distinct sources: food and sunlight. Relatively few foods contain vitamin D and all are of animal origin. The best sources are fish liver oils, fatty fish, milk, butter and margarine, eggs, cheese and liver. Sunlight on the skin results in the formation of vitamin D in the body.

Function

Vitamin D is concerned with the absorption of calcium in the intestine and the laying down of calcium and phosphorus in bones and teeth.

Deficiency

Deficiency of vitamin D is accompanied by the biochemical effects of calcium deficiency: **rickets**. This disease is common in people consuming poor diets. It used to be associated with slum dwellings where there was little sunlight. In recent years, cases have been recorded in the Asian community.

In adults an inadequate supply of vitamin D causes osteomalacia, a condition in which the bones become soft, weak and painful.

Effect of cooking processes

Minimal.

Vitamin E

Sources

It is found in small amounts in many foods, but rich sources are vegetables oils, wheatgerm, some margarines, eggs, wholemeal cereals and broccoli.

Functions

Vitamin E is found in all cell membranes and is thought to act as an antioxidant, i.e. it helps prevent the oxidation of fatty substances and so the breakdown of the cell walls in the body. It is thought that vitamin E may be important in the prevention of certain types of cancer.

Vitamin E also acts as an antioxidant in foods. It delays the development of rancidity caused by oxidation of fats and oils.

Deficiency

Deficiency of vitamin E is very rare because it is so widespread in foods. However, some premature infants require extra vitamin E, amongst other vitamins. Deficiency of vitamin E causes infertility in rats but there is little evidence of this in humans.

Effects of cooking processes

Unaffected by normal cooking processes except during prolonged frying processes.

Water soluble vitamins

Information about the water soluble vitamins is given in Table 4. More detailed information is included about vitamin C.

	Main Functions	Rich Sources	Effect of Cooking Processes
Vitamin B$_1$ (Thiamin)	Release of energy from food. Severe deficiency results in beri-beri. Rare in the UK	Milk, flour, bread, fortified cereals, meat, potatoes	Variable. Up to 50% loss in meat cookery, 25% loss in vegetable cookery
Vitamin B$_2$ (Riboflavin)	Release of energy from food. Deficiency results in stunted growth in children, cracks and sores in the corner of the mouth, swollen red tongue, misty eyes. Rare in the UK	Milk, eggs, green vegetables, beer, yeast	Small losses in cooking but is destroyed by U.V. light (e.g. milk in clear bottles)
Niacin (Nicotinic acid, Nicotinamide)	Release of energy from food. Deficiency rare in the UK. Causes retarded growth in children, sore skin and tongue and mental symptoms such as dementia. In severe cases pellagra develops	Widely distributed. Meat (especially offal), fish, whole-grain cereals, pulses	Minimal
Vitamin B$_6$ (Pyridoxine)	Protein and fat metabolism, red blood cell formation	Meat, liver, vegetables, bran	Minimal
Vitamin B$_{12}$ (Cyanocobala min)	Fat, protein and carbohydrate metabolism, red blood cell formation. Deficiency seen in strict vegetarians and vegans. Develop a type of anaemia	Animal products only; liver, meat, fish, eggs, milk	Minimal
Folic Acid (Folate)	Formation of red blood cells. Deficiency results in a type of anaemia, rare in the UK. Appears to have a role in prevention of neural tube defects such as spina bifida	Liver, leafy green vegetables, fish, pulses	Minimal
Pantothenic Acid	Healthy skin, growth and antibody production, metabolism of fat and carbohydrate	Liver, yeast, kidney, egg yolk, cereals	Minimal
Biotin	Healthy skin, forms part of several enzyme systems in metabolism	Egg yolk, liver, kidney, yeast	Minimal
Vitamin C (Ascorbic Acid)	Formation of connective tissue, helps absorption of iron. Deficiency seen as bleeding of gums, poor wound healing. Results in scurvy. Severe deficiency is rare but low blood and body tissue levels are common	Citrus fruits, currants, berries, green vegetables	Can result in loss of all the Vitamin C if proper procedures are not followed

Table 4: Water soluble vitamins

Vitamin C (Ascorbic acid)

Sources

Citrus fruit, currants, berries and fully grown green vegetables are the richest sources of vitamin C. Although root vegetables and potatoes contain relatively small proportions, they are important sources of the vitamin in the British diet because we eat so much of them.

Function

Vitamin C is concerned in a complex way with the structure of connective tissue which 'binds' the body cells together. It helps with the absorption of iron from the diet.

Deficiency

Scurvy was the scourge of the early mariners as their fresh rations ran out. It is seen as bleeding of the gums and hair follicles, failure of wounds to heal and eventually death. Although scurvy is rare in the UK, low blood and body tissue levels of vitamin C are more common and are associated with slow wound healing and similar problems.

Effect of cooking processes

Vitamin C is very unstable and great care is needed in food preparation to retain vitamin C. All plant cells contain the enzyme 'oxidase' and when released (e.g. during chopping of fruit and vegetables) it destroys vitamin C. There is a 5% loss of vitamin C with careful handling and 50% loss or more in careless handling.

Vitamin C is also 'leached' out into water used for cooking and heat also further destroys the vitamin. Reheated foods lose more vitamin C: on average 25% loss after 15 minutes, 75% loss after 90 minutes and longer storage of fruit and vegetables at 'warm' temperatures can result in almost 100% loss.

Rapid freezing after blanching is better than any other method at retaining vitamin C (blanching destroys the oxidase enzyme)

Recommendations	Reasons
Storage 1 Store in a cool, dark place. 2 Avoid bruising or damaging fruits and vegetables.	The rate of oxidation is increased by heat and light. Bruising damages the cells and releases the enzyme.
Preparation 1 Prepare just before cooking. 2 Do not soak in cold water. 3 Do not cut or chop more than necessary. 4 Tear rather than cut green leaves. 5 Avoid the use of iron (non-stainless) knives, graters, etc.	The enzyme is released when the cells are cut. Vitamin C is very water soluble. The enzyme is released when the cells are cut. Tearing causes the leaves to break around the cells. Iron increases the rate of oxidation.
Cooking 1 Place in boiling water. 2 Use a minimum quantity of water and a covered pan. 3 Do not overcook. 4 Do not add sodium bicarbonate to green vegetables.	The enzyme is destroyed by heat. Vitamin C leaches into cooking water; the greater the volume of water, the greater the vitamin C loss. Prolonged heating increases the amount of oxidation. Alkalis increase the rate of oxidation.
Service 1 Serve immediately; do not keep in hot cabinets for long periods of time. 2 Avoid mashing and puréeing unless there is some other ascorbic acid source to balance the menu.	Keeping hot for 45 minutes reduces vitamin C by 50% or more. Mashing and puréeing increase the rate of oxidation.

Table 5: Recommended methods of minimising vitamin C losses in vegetables and fruit

As far as nutritionists are concerned, the vitamins discussed in this section are the only 'true' vitamins for which we have good, reliable scientific information.

SELF CHECK QUESTIONS

---

1   *List four fat soluble vitamins.*
2   *List nine water soluble vitamins.*
3   *Why is it important not to overdose on fat soluble vitamins?*
4   *Give two reasons why vitamin C loss occurs during the preparation and cooking of fruits and vegetables.*

MINERALS

By the end of this section you should be able to
- list the major minerals and the trace elements
- state the main food sources of the major minerals
- understand the effect of over and under consumption of individual minerals

Introduction

Apart from hydrogen, carbon and oxygen (the main elements of which protein, fat and carbohydrate are composed) the body also requires around 20 other elements for a variety of reasons. Fifteen of them are known to be essential and a further three or more are necessary for normal life in other animal species and may prove to be necessary for man: no dietary deficiency has yet been shown.

Minerals have four main functions:

◆ body building e.g. constituents of bones and teeth
◆ control of body processes,e.g. transmission of nerve impulses
◆ essential part of body fluids and cells
◆ form part of many enzymes and other proteins which are necessary for the release and utilisation of energy.

Some mineral elements are required in relatively large amounts and are known as major minerals. These include:

1 **Major Minerals:**

Calcium	Sodium
Phosphorus	Chloride
Magnesium	Potassium
Iron	Zinc
Sulphur	

Others are required in minute amounts and are known as trace elements.

2 **Trace Elements:**

Iodine	Fluoride
Copper	Molybdenum
Cobalt	Sulphur
Chromium	Selenium
Manganese	

Major minerals

Information about the various minerals is given in Table 6 on page 23. More detail is included about calcium, iron and sodium because of concerns about consuming too little or too much of these.

Calcium

Sources

Calcium is found in good supply in milk, bones of canned fish, cheese, hard water and bread (added to white flour by law).

It is also found in green vegetables, but may be less available to the body. This is because fibre, which the body cannot digest, can affect calcium absorption. Similarly, it is found in whole grain cereals, but it may combine with a substance called phytic acid which makes it less available to the body.

Functions

◆ it combines with phosphorus to make calcium phosphate, which is the material that gives hardness and strength to bones and teeth. 99% of the body's calcium is stored in bones and teeth
◆ required for part of the complex mechanism which causes blood to clot after an injury
◆ required for the correct functioning of muscles and nerves.

	Main Functions	Rich Sources
Calcium	Growth and development of bones and teeth; blood clotting and hormone secretion	Milk, cheese, yoghurt, flour, bread, green vegetables, canned fish
Iron	Red blood cell formation; oxygen transport and transfer. Deficiency can lead to anaemia	Red meat (particularly offal), bread, flour and cereal products, green leaf vegetables
Sodium	Maintenance of constant body water content, muscle and nerve activity. High intakes have been related to high blood pressure	Table and cooking salt, bread, cereal products, meat products
Phosphorus	Component of all cells; combines with other minerals (eg. calcium) to give strength to bones and teeth	Milk, milk products, bread, cereal products, meat, meat products
Magnesium	Muscle tone; activation of enzymes – especially in protein synthesis	Milk, bread, cereal products, potatoes, other vegetables
Chloride	Assists sodium and potassium	Table and cooking salt, bread, cereal products, meat products, milk
Potassium	Maintenance of constant body water content	Vegetables, meat, milk, fruit and fruit juices
Zinc	Bone metabolism; activation of enzymes; release of Vitamin A; growth; immune system; taste; insulin release	Meat and meat products, meat, eggs, fish
Sulphur	Component of certain essential amino acids; metabolism of drugs; bone metabolism	Protein containing foods

Table 6: Major minerals

Requirements

The absorption of calcium (and phosphorus) and the mineralisation of bones and teeth are controlled by vitamin D. The body must have a sufficient supply of all three for it to function properly. Children need calcium for growth of bones and teeth. Pregnant women need extra calcium for the growth of the baby and for the maintenance of their own bones and teeth.

Deficiency

1 **Children**   Bones are not mineralised properly, and hence are not properly formed. The leg bones may bend under the weight of the body as rickets develops (this is not due to deficiency of calcium alone – see vitamin D, pages 17–18). Certain ethnic groups are at risk of deficiency e.g. Asians; the reasons for this are not completely understood.

2 **Adults**   Strength of bones and teeth is not maintained, possibly resulting in osteomalacia (adult rickets). In this country, rickets and osteomalacia are unlikely to be caused by low levels of calcium in the diet as the body can adapt to a lower level of intake. The primary deficiency is usually of vitamin D, and as a result too little calcium is absorbed.

3 **Senior citizens**   With increasing age the skeleton becomes weaker, and bone breakages occur more easily. This is known as osteoporosis – loss of bone. It is becoming increasingly common in our society. One in three women and one in ten men suffer fractures associated with this condition. The reasons for the increase are not understood – it is not simply the result of low calcium or vitamin D intakes.

Iron

Iron is a component of haemoglobin, the substance which gives red blood cells their colour. Haemoglobin is required to transport oxygen around the body to every cell; oxygen is needed for the production of energy and the maintenance of all cell functions.

Sources

Good sources are liver, kidney, corned beef, other red meat, cocoa, plain chocolate. Vitamin C helps absorption, therefore it is a good idea to eat vitamin C and iron rich foods together. However, tannin (found in tea) inhibits absorption.

Special requirements

1 **Infants**   Babies are born with a supply of iron to last them about three to six months as breast milk contains very little iron.

2 **Pregnant women**   Iron requirements are increased in pregnancy to allow for the development of the growing baby's blood supply. The proportion of iron absorbed from the diet increases in pregnancy, but iron tablets are sometimes recommended.

3   **Girls and women**   The regular menstrual loss of blood means that iron is lost and must be replaced. It is estimated that 30% of European women are iron deficient.

4   **Injuries and operations**   These result in loss of blood, and the iron must therefore be replaced.

Deficiency

Deficiency results in haemoglobin not being made properly, so insufficient oxygen is carried around the body. This leads to tiredness, weakness, and a pale complexion. In severe cases this leads to iron deficiency, **anaemia**. General health is affected as cells cannot function properly.

Anaemia in infants and young children

There is evidence that anaemia in older infants and toddlers is quite widespread. This is one reason for recommending the use of fortified infant formula milk until at least one year of age, as cow's milk is a poor source of iron. Iron fortified cereals may also be of benefit although the proportion of the iron that is absorbed is not known. Iron rich foods should be included in the diet of all young children.

Sodium

Sodium is of vital importance in maintaining a constant body water content and is also essential for muscle and nerve activity.

Excess sodium is excreted through the kidney since it is essential that the sodium and chloride balance in the blood is maintained within close limits. The quantity of sodium gained from food is balanced by an equivalent loss in the urine. Some sodium may also be lost in sweat but this is only significant after strenuous exercise or in hot climates. Although adaptation can occur, extra salt may occasionally be needed to prevent muscle cramps. In temperate climates the amount of salt needed by an adult is less than 3g per day but we consume on average 9g per day.

High intakes over long periods may lead to raised blood pressure in susceptible adults and hence we are advised to consume less salt.

Trace minerals

These are essential to the body in small quantities. Deficiency is either rare or not observed as they are usually present in a wide range of foods. Excess levels of trace minerals are toxic. Information about the trace minerals is given in Table 7 below.

	Main Functions	Rich Sources
Iodine	Constituent of thyroid hormones, which regulate many body processes	Milk and milk products, meat, eggs, fish
Copper	Growth; component of many enzymes – including those needed for formation of blood and bone – and in the body's defence system; neurotransmittor function; cell respiration	Wholegrain cereals, meat, vegetables
Cobalt	Component of Vitamin B_{12}	Animal products
Chromium	Enhances the action of insulin, which controls the utilisation of glucose	Widely distributed, particularly wholegrain cereals and vegetables
Manganese	Helps to maintain structure of cells; enzymes	Wholegrain cereals, nuts and tea
Selenium	Part of an enzyme involved in protection of membranes and lipids against oxidative damage	Cereals, fish, offal, meat, cheese, eggs, milk
Molybdenum	Component of several enzymes – including one concerned in the formation of uric acid; possibly in the utilisation of iron	Widely distributed, particularly in vegetables and pulses
Fluoride	Increases the resistance of teeth to decay	Tea, fish, water

Table 7: Trace minerals

SELF CHECK QUESTIONS

1   Name three foods that contain useful amounts of calcium.
2   State two functions of calcium in the body.
3   Why is it inadvisable to eat too much salt (sodium chloride)?
4   What medical condition arises if iron intakes are insufficient?
5   What is the function of iodine in the body?
6   Name two foods that contain useful amounts of zinc.

WATER

By the end of this section you should be able to
- understand why although water is not a nutrient, it is essential to life

Water balance

All living organisms contain water; the human body consists of about 65% water. It is the medium in which nutrients, enzymes and other chemical substances can be dispersed and in which the chemical reactions necessary for maintaining life take place. It is also necessary as a means of transport within the body. Nutrients are carried to cells and waste products are transported from the cells by blood plasma which is 90% water. It is possible to exist for several weeks without food, but the body can only survive a few days without water. Water comes from 'solid' foods as well as from drinks and is lost by evaporation in the breath and sweat as well as in the urine.

The balance of water retained in the body is normally very carefully regulated by the kidneys. Excessive losses can occur usually as a result of vomiting or diarrhoea, in illness or from heavy sweating due to strenuous activity or a hot climate. If water intake is not increased, dehydration may result.

The amount of water taken into the body is determined mainly by habit and social custom. It is also regulated by thirst which arises as a result of the concentration of sodium in the blood. The body cannot store water and any excess passes into the urine.

DIGESTION AND ABSORPTION

By the end of this section you should be able to
- understand the basic processes of digestion
- state the major sites of absorption of various nutrients
- state the ultimate fate of the various nutrients in the body

Introduction

Food taken into the mouth is useless to the body until it has been absorbed through the lining of the alimentary canal (digestive tract) and carried by the blood to the tissues. Digestion is the breakdown of the complex nutrient molecules in food into molecules small enough to be absorbed through the lining of the intestine. Certain components of food (monosaccharides, salts, water and alcohol) do not need to be digested since they are composed of small soluble molecules. Digestion is mainly a chemical process of hydrolysis (break down) which requires the presence of enzymes.

Enzymes are proteins which control all the chemical reactions in living organisms. Most enzymes are named by adding the suffix 'ase'. For example:

◆ Carbohydrases break down carbohydrates
◆ Lipases break down lipids
◆ Proteases break down proteins
◆ Hydrolases are involved in hydrolytic reactions.

Some enzymes (e.g. pepsin and rennin) still retain their original names. The nutrients hydrolysed by digestive enzymes are:

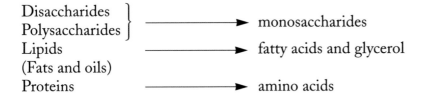

Disaccharides ⎫
Polysaccharides ⎬ ──────────▶ monosaccharides

Lipids ──────────▶ fatty acids and glycerol
(Fats and oils)

Proteins ──────────▶ amino acids

Digestion is also in part a physical process. Food particles are reduced in size by the grinding and chewing action of teeth and by the muscular action of the alimentary canal.

Alimentary canal

The digestive tract is basically a tube about eight metres long, open at both ends: see Figure 4.

Mouth

Food is broken into smaller pieces by the grinding and chewing action of the teeth (mastication). At the sight, smell and taste of food the salivary glands are stimulated and a steady flow of saliva enters the mouth. Saliva is composed of water together with:

1   **Mucin**: a slimy, protein containing substance which lubricates food and makes it easier to swallow.

2   **Salivary amylase**: an enzyme which starts the breakdown of starch into maltose. Food is mixed with saliva and reduced to a soft mass or bolus by

the action of the tongue and jaws before it is swallowed. After being swallowed it is carried down the oesophagus by peristalsis, rhythmic contractions of the muscles in the wall of the oesophagus.

No significant absorption of nutrients occurs through the lining of the mouth.

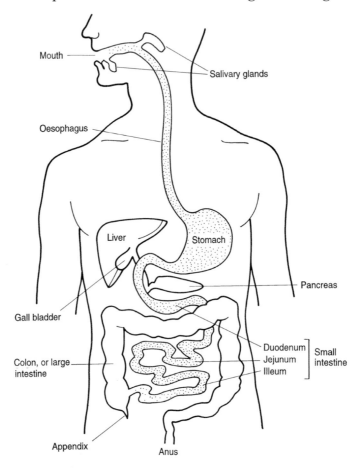

Figure 4: The Digestive Tract

Stomach

The stomach acts as a reservoir, so that rather than eating continually, food need only be consumed at intervals. The cells lining the stomach produce gastric juice. Secretion of gastric juice is stimulated by the sight, smell and taste of food and also by the presence of food in the stomach. Gastric juice contains:

1   **pepsin**: an enzyme which breaks down some proteins into smaller molecules called polypeptides.

2   **hydrochloric acid**: which activates pepsin and kills bacteria.

3   **rennin**: an enzyme which coagulates milk protein, important only in babies.

4   **intrinsic factor**: a substance needed for the absorption of vitamin B_{12}.

Waves of muscular contractions in the stomach walls mix the food with the gastric juice, producing a mixture known as chyme. Food normally remains in the stomach for two to four hours.

At intervals small portions of chyme pass through a valve called the pyloric sphincter into the small intestine.

Some simple substances can pass through the lining of the stomach into the blood stream in small quantities. This includes water, alcohol, simple sugars and water soluble vitamins.

Small intestine

Most of the various digestive processes take place in the small intestine. As chyme enters the duodenum, the first part of the small intestine, it is acted on by three digestive juices:

1   **pancreatic juice** is produced in the pancreas, and contains enzymes which continue the digestion of proteins, starch and fats.

2   **bile** is a yellow brown fluid produced in the liver and stored in the gall bladder. The presence of fat and other foods in the small intestine brings about contraction of the gall bladder and the flow of bile into the small intestine. Bile contains bile salts which aid fat digestion.

3   **intestinal juice** is secreted by the cells lining the small intestine and contains:

<u>a</u>   **peptidases**: a group of enzymes which complete the breakdown of proteins by splitting polypeptides into amino acids; and

<u>b</u>   **disaccharide splitting enzymes**: maltase, sucrase and lactase which hydrolyse maltose, sucrose and lactose into their respective monosaccharides.

Absorption of almost all nutrients takes place along the whole length of the small intestine. The process of absorption is very efficient. The inner lining of the wall is folded into finger-like projections called **villi**, which provide a very large surface area (20–40 square metres) for absorption. Any food which is not digested and absorbed passes into the large intestine.

Large intestine (colon)

The main function of the large intestine is to remove water from the fluid mixture which enters from the small intestine. Water is absorbed through the lining of the colon so that undigested food leaves the body in a semi-solid state. The large intestine contains a very large number of bacteria which break down some of the cellulose and other components of undigested food using their own enzyme. Some of these bacteria can synthesise certain vitamins; e.g. some B vitamins and vitamin K. The vitamins can be absorbed into the blood stream.

Undigested food materials, residues from digestive juices, dead cells from the lining of the alimentary canal, bacteria and water form the faeces which are passed out of the body through the anus.

What happens to major nutrients in the body?

Carbohydrates

The simple sugars entering the intestinal wall are carried by the blood stream directly to the liver. They may then be:

◆ passed as glucose to all the cells of the body to be used directly for energy
◆ converted into glycogen and stored in the liver and skeletal muscles as a readily available source of energy
◆ converted into fatty acids and stored in the body fat (adipose tissue) as a source of energy.

Fats

Almost all the fatty acids which enter the intestinal wall are immediately rebuilt into triglycerides which are carried to the blood stream by lymph. Fat may be further transformed by the liver and some of it is finally deposited in the adipose tissue. The reservoir of fat is constantly available as a source of energy.

Proteins

When the peptides enter the intestinal wall, they are split into amino acids which are carried in the blood directly to the liver. Then:

◆ they may be passed into the general circulation where they enter the body's 'pool' of essential and non-essential amino acids. These are then built into the structural proteins and specific enzymes which each cell needs

◆ the excess of some amino acids may be converted into those that are lacking
◆ any excess of amino acids will be used as a source of energy or converted to body fat.

SELF CHECK QUESTIONS

---

1   *Name three areas of the alimentary canal where digestion occurs.*
2   *Name two enzymes that help in the digestion of disaccharides.*
3   *Where in the alimentary canal are most nutrients absorbed?*

FOOD AND ENERGY

By the end of this section you should be able to
- state which components of food provide energy
- know the three main uses of energy in the body

Energy value of nutrients

All living organisms require a source of energy. The chemical energy in food is released in the cells of animals by oxidation. Some of the energy is used to maintain metabolic processes in the cells, some is converted into heat to maintain body temperature and some is converted into mechanical energy which is used for physical activity.

The unit of energy is the **joule**. Since the joule is too small for practical nutrition the kilojoule (kJ) is used. However, traditionally the **Calorie** or more correctly, the **kilocalorie (kcal)** unit was used and so normally energy values are given in both types of unit.

$$1 \text{ kilocalorie (1kcal)} = 4.18\text{kJ}$$

An even larger unit, the **megajoule (MJ)** is also used:

$$1\text{MJ} = 1{,}000{,}000 \text{ joules}$$
$$= 1000\text{kJ}$$

The three groups of nutrients which provide the body with energy are carbohydrates, fats and proteins.

◆ 1g of carbohydrate provides 3.75kcal (16kJ)
◆ 1g of fat provides 9kcal (37kJ)
◆ 1g of protein provides 4.0kcal (17kJ)

If alcohol is consumed this also contributes to the body's energy intake.

◆ 1g of alcohol provides 7kcal (29kJ)

Energy value of foods

The energy value of food, often called the Calorie content, depends on the quantities of carbohydrate, fat and protein (and sometimes alcohol) in the food. The total energy value of a food in Calories will be the total of the amount of Carbohydrate (g) ×3.75, Protein (g) ×4, Fat (g) ×9 plus Alcohol(g) ×7. If the energy value is required in kJ then the kJ conversion factors given above will need to be used.

Use of energy by the body

1 **Basal Metabolism**   This is the term used to describe the basic metabolic processes which keep the body alive. Energy is needed to keep the heart beating and the lungs functioning, to maintain body temperature and muscle tone and for the numerous chemical reactions taking place in body cells. The rate at which energy is used up in maintaining basal metabolism is called basal metabolic rate (BMR).

2 **Physical Activity**   In addition to basal metabolism, energy is used by the body for muscular activity. The energy requirements for various

Activity	kcal/min
Sitting	1.4
Writing	1.7
Standing	1.7
Washing-up	2.4
Domestic work	2.9
Walking	3.3– 5.0
Running	6.0–15.6
Tennis	4.8– 8.4
Football	4.8– 8.4
Swimming	4.8–12

Table 8: Energy consumption of various activities

activities have been determined by measuring oxygen uptake during different activities.

Although these figures are not accurate for any individual, they provide useful comparisons.

3   **Growth, Pregnancy and Lactation**   Additional energy is needed during growth to provide for the extra body tissue. During pregnancy and lactation all the infant's needs for energy must be supplied by the mother. Up to 80,000 kcal of extra food energy may be needed during pregnancy, mostly during the final months.

4   **Heat**   Some of the energy in food will be used as a source of heat, some of which will be used to keep the body warm.

The dietary energy required by an individual who is neither gaining nor losing weight exactly equals the energy expended on maintenance and physical activity. In practice this balance is achieved over periods of a few days with remarkable accuracy.

A man might expend 2,550 kcal in a typical day as follows:

	kcal
8 hours asleep	530
8 hours at work	
6 hr sitting	500
2 hr standing/walking	300
8 hours non-occupational activities	
2 hr 15 min travelling	270
15 min washing/dressing	50
1.5 hr light domestic duties	270
3 hr sitting, eating, reading, watching TV	250
30 min squash	230
30 min gardening	<u>150</u>
	2550

Because of individual variations, the diet of any particular person may provide more or less energy than this.

Having considered the nutrients we need to consume and how the body obtains them from food, the next chapter looks at what types of foods and diets we should be eating.

SELF CHECK QUESTIONS

1   *Name four components of food that provide energy.*
2   *Which nutrient supplies the most energy per gram?*
3   *State four uses of energy in the body.*

What Should we be Eating?

Having considered all the nutrients we need to eat, this chapter is concerned with food. Most people do not think about nutrients when they are planning what to eat; instead they think about food. Getting the correct balance of foods in our diet should ensure we consume adequate but not excessive amounts of individual nutrients. This is the aim of dietary guidelines which are discussed in this chapter. Clearly, eating a good diet is an important part of our overall health and this is recognised in the Government's Health of the Nation initiative which aims to improve further the health of people living in the UK. The role of caterers in helping to achieve the diet and nutrition targets, and hence improving diet in this country, is also discussed.

DIETARY GUIDELINES

By the end of this section you should be able to
- describe the current dietary guidelines
- understand the term Dietary Reference Values
- explain the uses of Dietary Reference Values

Introduction

The aim of dietary guidelines is to help people choose a diet that contains the foods they need for good health. If the guidelines are followed, the diet should contain all the nutrients the body needs in the right amounts. The guidelines should also help in the prevention of so-called diet-related diseases such as Coronary Heart Disease. Although we know quite a lot about what nutrients we need, most people don't think or know about nutrients; they just eat the food! Dietary guidelines do not however tell you exactly what to eat; there are thousands of ways of eating a good diet.

Current dietary guidelines

A number of organisations have put forward dietary guidelines over recent years. The most recent advice is found in *The National Food Guide: The Balance of Good Health*. This guide was published in 1994 and is reproduced below.

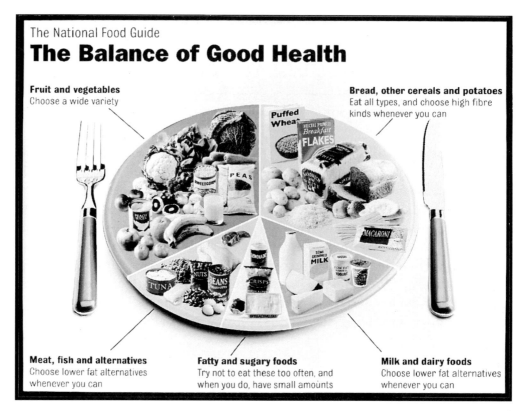

Figure 5: The Balance of Good Health
Reproduced with permission of the Health Education Authority

The plate is divided into five sections, representing the five food groups. The sizes of the segments represent the proportion of the diet that the foods should contribute. The largest part of the diet should come from two of the five groups.

1   **Bread, other cereals and potatoes**   This group provides carbohydrates, non-starch polysaccharides (fibre), B group vitamins, calcium and iron.

2   **Fruit and vegetables**   The foods in this group are good sources of many vitamins and minerals as well as non-starch polysaccharides.

Smaller amounts of the diet should come from next two groups.

3   **Meat, fish and alternatives**   This group provides protein as well as iron, other minerals and B group vitamins.

4   **Milk and dairy foods**   The dairy group provides calcium, protein and other minerals and vitamins.

The last group contains non-essential food items.

5   **Fatty and sugary foods**   Only small amounts of foods should come
from this group as they contain large amounts of fat and/or sugar and are
often high in energy (Calories). At the same time, they are low in
essential nutrients. The foods in this group are not essential and should
be eaten infrequently in small amounts.

What this means is that most people will need to eat fewer foods with a high
fat, sugar and salt content and more foods with a high fibre content.

The Balance of Good Health applies to most people, but not to very young
children or some people under medical supervision, or who have special dietary
requirements. The guide can be used by individual consumers, food producers,
manufacturers and caterers.

Another advantage of having a guide is that the argument that 'they' are always
changing their minds about what we should be eating can be easily dismissed.
In fact the types of food we are being advised to eat now is very similar to what
has been recommended for many years. The Guide should help in getting the
right advice to everyone.

The Guide is not the only source of dietary guidelines in the UK. Other
information is available (for details see publications listed in Appendix 1, page
198).

EXERCISE

Write down everything you ate and drank over the last 24 hours.
Compare it with *The Balance of Good Food* and answer the following
questions.
1   Did you eat foods from all 5 groups?
    If not, which group(s) were missing?
2   Were the amounts of foods you ate in the recommended
    proportions?
3   What changes would you need to make to bring your diet into line
    with the Guide?

How were the dietary guidelines devised?

In 1991 a government committee called the Committee on Medical Aspects of
Food Policy published a report entitled **Dietary Reference Values**. It contains
details of the amounts of the various nutrients we need to consume. For many
years before this we had published figures of the amounts of energy and

nutrients needed by the UK population. You may be familiar with the Recommended Daily Amounts. As we now know more about nutrient requirements and the relationship between diet and disease, these figures needed updating, and this is what is included in the Dietary Reference Values report.

The report provides details of the range of nutrient requirements likely to be found in the UK population. A very wide range of vitamins and minerals are included, and recommendations for the amount of fat, carbohydrate and non-starch polysaccharide (dietary fibre) are included for the first time.

The Dietary Reference Values (DRVs) can be used for the following purposes:

◆ to assess the adequacy of the diets of individuals and groups of people
◆ calculating the nutritional content of meals and menus
◆ for planning food supplies.

The DRVs for the energy providing nutrients are as follows:

◆ FAT   35% of total energy, with no more than 11% from saturated fat
◆ PROTEIN   15% of total energy
◆ CARBOHYDRATE   50% of total energy (39% from starch, 11% from non-milk extrinsic sugar (sucrose))

Appendix 2 gives details of other Dietary Reference Values you are likely to find useful.

In order to be able to use these figures for assessing meals, you will need to find out the energy and nutrient content of the meal. This can be achieved by using nutritional information in *The Composition of Foods* (see Useful Publications list, page 198). Computer software is available to increase the speed at which you can carry out this type of analysis. Once you know the amount of nutrients your meal contains, you can compare the results with the DRV figures. You will then be able to make suggestions on how the meal could be amended to meet the dietary guidelines more closely, if this is necessary.

EXERCISE

1   Calculate the energy, protein, fat and carbohydrate content of the following recipe, using *The Composition of Foods*.
    700g rump steak
    100g onion
    75g butter
    400g mushrooms
    150g double cream

EXERCISE

In order to compare your results with the Dietary Reference Values, you will need to carry out the following calculations. This is because the recommendations for fat, carbohydrate and protein are given as percentages of the amount of energy (Calories). Your calculations will be in grams. In order to convert you will need to use the following information.

◆ 1 gram of fat provides the body with 9kcals
◆ multiply the grams of fat in your meal × 9
(this will tell you how many kcal come from fat)
◆ divide this figure into the total kcal in your meal
◆ multiply your answer × 100
(this will give you the percentage of the total energy that is coming from fat).

For example if your meal contains 20g of fat and provides 300kcals the calculation will be as follows:

20g × 9 = 180 (the amount of energy (kcal) coming from fat)

$\dfrac{180}{300}$ × 100 = 60% (this means that 60% of the kcals in your recipe come from fat which is much higher than the 35% recommended)

The calculations for carbohydrate will be the same *except* that 1 gram of carbohydrate provides the body with 3.75kcal.
For protein, 1 gram of protein provides the body with 4kcal.
(See Chapter 1 for more information about the energy value of food.)

2   Once you have calculated this information you can compare your results with the DRV for fat, carbohydrate and protein (see Appendix 2, page 202).

3   Make suggestions as to how you would change the recipe to make it 'healthier'.

The procedure for assessing the adequacy of diets is similar to that outlined above. If any alcohol is included then you will need to consult the Dietary Reference Values Report as the figures for fat and other nutrients are slightly different.

The DRV report provides a firm scientific basis on which to base good dietary advice. It does not attempt to provide the perfect diet. It needed to be translated into a more 'user friendly' format that considered foods, not nutrients. The aim of *The Balance of Good Health* was to translate these recommendations about nutrients into guidance about food choice.

SELF CHECK QUESTIONS

---

1   *What are the five food groups in The Balance of Good Health?*
2   *For each of the groups name two nutrients that the foods provide in significant amounts.*
3   *Give three uses of the Dietary Reference Values.*

THE HEALTH OF THE NATION INITIATIVE

By the end of this section you should be able to
- explain why we have The Health of the Nation initiative
- understand the role of the Nutrition Task Force and related committees

In addition to the reports mentioned so far there is one other that is relevant to a discussion of diet and health in the UK. This is The Health of the Nation White Paper published in 1992. For the first time in England, it established a comprehensive strategy for promoting public health across the whole community. Similar initiatives are taking place in Scotland, Wales and Northern Ireland.

The Health of the Nation strategy aims to secure a continual improvement in the general health of the population 'not just by adding years to life but also by adding life to years'. The intention is for everyone to live longer and also to spend their additional years as free as possible from ill health.

The strategy was based on the idea that all organisations concerned with health would work with each other including government, education, health professionals and the media.

Five key areas were identified for immediate action:

◆ Coronary Heart Disease and Stroke
◆ Cancers

◆ Mental health
◆ HIV/AIDS and sexual health
◆ Accidents.

In the key area of Coronary heart disease (CHD) and Stroke, targets were set for reductions in the death rate from both these conditions by the year 2000. It was recognised that for these targets to be met, changes in diet would be needed (amongst other things). Hence diet-related targets were set. Most of the figures that were used came from the DRV report, but dates by which the targets should be met were also included (Appendix 3 contains further details).

Following on from the publication of the White Paper, a whole range of programmes of action have been implemented. In order to help achieve the diet-related targets, the Nutrition Task Force was established. The Task Force drew together a wide range of expertise from food manufacturing, retailing, caterers, health professionals, consumers and the media, to work with government departments. Action was considered in four areas: catering, education and information, the food chain, and the National Health Service and health professionals. One result of this initiative was the production of *The Balance of Good Food* discussed earlier. There have been many other reports and guidelines produced for all those individuals and organisations concerned with food.

The Health of the Nation initiative is important because it is the first time that such a wide ranging but integrated approach has been taken to health prevention in this country.

ROLE OF CATERERS IN THE DIET IN THE UK

By the end of this section you should able to
● explain why caterers need to be concerned about the nutritional content of the meals and menus they provide

The number of meals eaten outside the home is continually increasing. This includes restaurants, pubs, clubs, fast-food establishments and sandwich bars. The amount of money spent on catering is rising faster than the rate of inflation. Between 1984 and 1994 the proportion of total consumer expenditure spent on catering increased from 6.3% to 8.7%.

A survey of British adults found that on average, a quarter of their food intake was eaten out of the home. This means that for some people a large proportion of their food intake is eaten outside the home. Remember, eating out of the home does not just include visits to restaurants and trips to fast food establishments. In some situations caterers provide all meals for people, such as in hospitals, prisons or the Armed Forces. Similarly the meal may play an important role in the overall diet, e.g. school meals, work place canteens and Meals on Wheels.

The nutritional content of meals provided by the caterers can therefore be extremely important. The old argument that eating out is an irregular activity and the contribution to overall diets is small is no longer valid. As well as having an obligation to provide safe, nutritious meals, caterers are facing demand from customers as concern about diet and health increases. Customers want to eat healthily but they also want food to look and taste good. The result is that the way meals are produced and the types of foods used may need to be changed.

The Health of the Nation White Paper acknowledges the important role that caterers have to play in helping to improve diet and the health of the public at large. Methods of achieving this aim are outlined in the next chapter.

SELF CHECK QUESTIONS

1   *Give three reasons why caterers should be concerned about the nutritional content of the meals they produce.*
2   *What is the main aim of the Health of the Nation initiative?*
3   *Why was the Nutrition Task force set up?*

Nutrition Problems in Today's Society

This chapter looks at the nutrition problems that affect large numbers of people in our society. Coronary Heart Disease (CHD), certain types of cancer, obesity, being overweight and conditions associated with lack of fibre in the diet are extremely common. The role of diet in all of these problems is discussed below, followed by a section on how caterers can help to improve the nation's diet.

In many ways health in the UK today is better than it has ever been. Many infectious diseases have been brought under control and some almost eliminated. As can be seen from the figure below infant deaths rates have declined from over 150 per 1000 live births to less than 10. We are also living longer. Men now live for an average of 73 years compared with 44 years only 100 years ago: see Figures 6 and 7 on page 46.

In addition each generation of children is taller than their parents. Some, but not all, of these changes are due to improvements in diet. So what are the nutrition problems we should be concerned with today?

In order to investigate this it is useful to look at the major causes of death in this country and compare them with 60 years ago: see Figure 8 on page 47.

Clearly the major change is in the increase in the proportion of deaths from circulatory diseases (which include Coronary Heart Disease and Stroke) and the decrease in deaths from infectious diseases. Although all the causes of heart disease are not completely understood it is known that the type of diet we eat is important. Secondly, cancer is now the second major cause of death and it is estimated that 35% of cancers are related to diet.

Another worrying statistic that does not appear on the diagram is the increase in the number of people who are overweight and obese. Half of the adult population in this country fit into this category and the number is increasing. Obesity and being overweight contribute to an increased risk of a whole range of conditions including CHD and cancer, as well as making other conditions like respiratory diseases more serious.

Nutrition is therefore a factor in all three of the major causes of death in this country. There are also other nutrition-related problems which affect health,

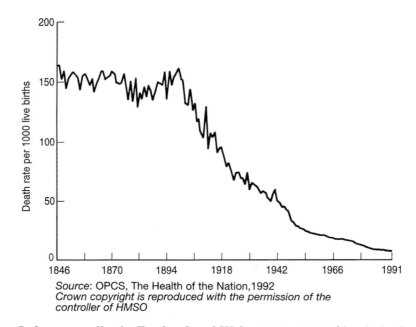

Source: OPCS, The Health of the Nation,1992
*Crown copyright is reproduced with the permission of the
controller of HMSO*

Figure 6: Infant mortality in England and Wales 1846–1991 (deaths in first year of life)

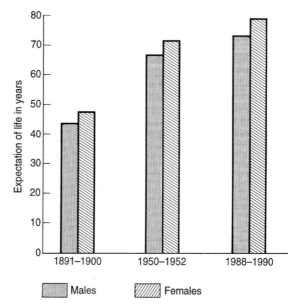

Source: Government Actuary's Department, The Health of the Nation, 1992
Crown copyright is reproduced with the permission of the controller of HMSO

Figure 7: Expectation of life at birth in England and Wales 1891 to 1952, and England 1988–1990

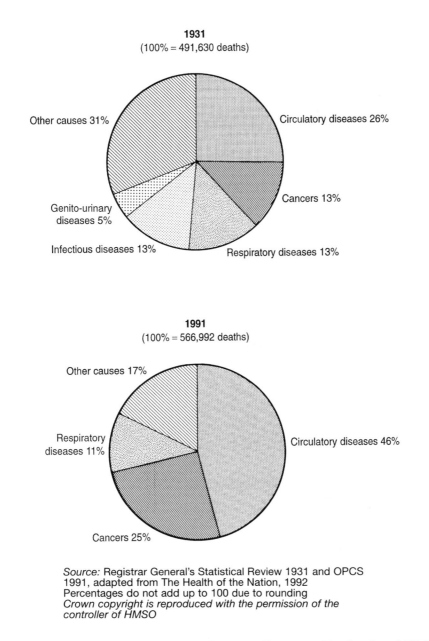

1931
(100% = 491,630 deaths)

Other causes 31%

Circulatory diseases 26%

Cancers 13%

Genito-urinary diseases 5%

Respiratory diseases 13%

Infectious diseases 13%

1991
(100% = 566,992 deaths)

Other causes 17%

Respiratory diseases 11%

Circulatory diseases 46%

Cancers 25%

Source: Registrar General's Statistical Review 1931 and OPCS
1991, adapted from The Health of the Nation, 1992
Percentages do not add up to 100 due to rounding
Crown copyright is reproduced with the permission of the
controller of HMSO

Figure 8: Major causes of death 1931 and 1991, all persons England and Wales
(data for 1991 excludes deaths of those aged under 28 days)

and although they don't usually result in death, can be very serious; e.g. bowel
disorders associated with lack of fibre in the diet and allergy to certain foods.
Finally there is concern about other components of food such as food additives.

This chapter will consider the nutrition problems and issues that affect large
numbers of people. The following chapter will consider the nutrition needs of
smaller groups within our population.

CORONARY HEART DISEASE AND STROKE

By the end of this section you should be able to
- explain the role of atheroma in heart disease and stroke
- understand the concept of risk factors
- describe the role of diet in CHD

Facts about Coronary Heart Disease and Stroke

◆ CHD is the leading cause of death in the UK. The number of people dying is more than the equivalent of a jumbo jet crashing and killing all passengers every day of the year.

◆ Coronary Heart Disease kills a lot of younger people. It is the biggest single cause of death amongst men before the age of 65.

◆ Men in Scotland and Northern Ireland have the worst rates of heart disease in the world; they have a ten times greater chance of dying before the age of 65 than men in Japan and four times greater than men in France.

◆ Death rates from CHD have fallen over the last 25 years but much larger decreases have been reported in the USA and Australia.

◆ A man with a manual job has three times the chance of dying prematurely from CHD than a man with a professional job like doctor or lawyer.

◆ Cigarette smoking is estimated to be responsible for 20% of CHD deaths.

What is Coronary Heart Disease?

Heart disease is the result of partial or complete blockage of the coronary arteries which take blood to the heart muscle. The arteries are narrowed by

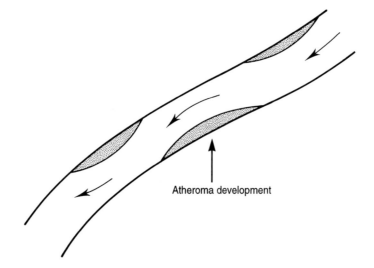

Atheroma development

Figure 9: Atheroma in an artery

fatty deposits called **atheroma** or plaque which develop on the artery wall. Atheroma consists of cholesterol, fatty deposits and cell wall material. It can take up to 30 years for atheroma to develop. Clearly blood has more difficulty flowing through an artery with atheroma than one without atheroma.

High levels of cholesterol in the blood appear to encourage the development of atheroma, and this is why many people have their blood cholesterol levels checked. If the level is high then the person will be given advice on how to try and reduce it.

High levels of blood cholesterol and/or the presence of atheroma do not result in heart disease on their own. Coronary heart diseases take two forms:

1   **Angina**   Because blood cannot flow freely through arteries affected by atheroma, the heart has to work harder to force the blood through. During exercise blood flow must be increased and the heart must work even harder, and as a result pain occurs.

2   **Heart Attack**   This results from a sudden severe blockage in the coronary artery. The blockage is usually a blood clot or thrombus. In a heart attack the heart muscle is starved of oxygen, causing damage to the heart muscle which causes pain. In a severe heart attack the muscle may be so badly damaged that the heart may stop beating. If the heart does not start beating again within a few minutes, death will result.

Clots can occur anywhere in the body. If one lodges in the brain the result will be a stroke. How severe the stroke is depends on what area of the brain is affected, but strokes can be fatal.

Risk factors for CHD

CHD is a multifactorial disease, i.e. there is not one single cause. A number of factors found in people who appear to be well, relate to the appearance of CHD. These risk factors only indicate that a person is more likely to get CHD, not that they definitely will.

There are four major risk factors:

◆ cigarette smoking
◆ high blood cholesterol concentration
◆ high blood pressure
◆ insufficient exercise.

Other factors are also important:

◆ middle age
◆ male sex
◆ family history
◆ stress
◆ obesity.

Some risk factors are related to diet, but others are clearly not. An individual cannot always control all factors, e.g. being male! In order to try and reduce the amount of heart disease, it is necessary to look at factors that can be controlled, like diet.

The role of diet in CHD

Medical evidence suggests that diets high in fat (particularly saturated fat) are linked to high levels of cholesterol in blood, which in turn affect the development of atheroma and the risk of developing heart disease and stroke. Because heart disease affects so many people and we cannot always predict who will be affected, we are all being recommended to eat less fat, particularly saturated fat.

Fat is not the only concern. The amount of salt we eat affects blood pressure in some individuals. High blood pressure increases the risk of both CHD and stroke and because we all eat much more salt than we need, we are being recommended to eat less of it. In addition, high intakes of alcohol can result in high blood pressure. Obesity is also a factor in heart disease. Obese people are much more likely to suffer from high blood pressure.

There is still a lot more for researchers to find out about diet and CHD. Recent evidence suggests that certain components of fruit and vegetables may help in the prevention of heart disease. Also, certain types of long chain polyunsaturated fatty acids (found mainly in fish oils) may help reduce the tendency of blood to clot and hence the risk of heart attacks or stroke.

Diet is not the only risk factor which can be modified. Stopping smoking and taking more exercise are also extremely important.

As CHD and stroke are such serious problems in our society, any attempt to improve the health of people in this country must include steps to help prevent these conditions developing. The Health of the Nation set targets for reducing CHD and stroke by the year 2000 by between 30–40% (see Appendix 3). Because diet is an important factor in heart disease, targets were also set for reducing fat, saturated fat and alcohol intakes, as well as for reducing obesity and high blood pressure.

Looking back at the dietary guidelines in Chapter 2, if people eat diets in line with *The Balance of Good Health* then their diet will be lower in fat, salt and sugar, and higher in starchy carbohydrates and fibre. This type of diet should help reduce the risk of developing CHD and also stroke.

SELF CHECK QUESTIONS

I   *What is atheroma?*
2   *What are the four major risk factors?*
3   *As well as fat, what other food components are believed to affect risk of CHD?*

CANCER

> By the end of this section you should be able to
> - explain the possible role of certain foods in cancer
> - describe the type of diet that may help prevent cancer

There is mounting medical and scientific evidence of a connection between what we eat and the likelihood of suffering from cancer some time in the future. It is estimated that 35% of all cancer deaths are related to diet. This does not mean that diet necessarily causes cancer, but what we eat may help promote or inhibit cancer development.

What is cancer?

Body cells are continually dividing in order for children to grow and to replace worn out cells in both adults and children. In cancer there is an overgrowth of body cells which eventually invade the rest of the body. It is known that certain environmental chemicals, viruses, radiation and asbestos cause cancer. Smoking and other uses of tobacco are responsible for an estimated 30% of all cancer deaths.

What do we know about diet and cancer?

The amount of fat that people eat has been linked to the chances of getting cancer. To reduce the risk, it is recommended we eat less fat. Obese people are more prone to certain types of cancer, and reducing the amount of fat eaten may help in reducing body weight.

Diets low in fruit, vegetables and whole grain cereals appear to increase the risk of developing cancer. Although a lot more research is needed in this area, there are a number of reasons why we should be eating more of these foods. They contain beta-carotene (which is converted to vitamin A in the body), vitamin C, vitamin E, the mineral Selenium and dietary fibre. All of these substances may have a role in preventing the development of cancer.

Eating large amounts of salted, pickled or smoked foods has been linked to certain types of cancer and hence these foods should be consumed in moderation.

Drinking alcohol appears to increase chances of developing certain types of cancer. In excessive amounts, especially combined with cigarette smoking, there is even more risk. The advice is therefore not to drink at all or to consume only small amounts.

The type of diet that is recommended to help prevent cancer is similar to that for preventing heart disease, although the reasons for increasing or decreasing certain types of food are different.

OBESITY AND OVERWEIGHT

At the end of this section you should be able to
- state how many people are overweight and obese in this country
- understand the use of Body Mass Index
- explain the difference between obesity and being overweight

Being overweight or obese is not, on its own, a common cause of death. However, as we have seen, it does increase the risk of CHD, stroke and certain types of cancer. In addition it increases the risk of diabetes and gallstones. The severity of many illnesses is increased by being overweight or obese, e.g. respiratory diseases and arthritis. Obese people are also more at risk of complications if they have to have surgery.

How is overweight and obesity defined?

It is now common to use the **Body Mass Index** (BMI) as an index of population fatness.

$$BMI = \frac{Weight}{Height^2}$$

(weight is measured in kilograms and height in metres)

The following classification system is used in many countries

BMI

20 or less	Underweight
20–25	Acceptable weight
25–30	Overweight
30–40	Obese
more than 40	Very obese

A BMI of 30 or more indicates obesity and it is at this point and above that there is significantly increased risk of the various conditions mentioned above.

EXERCISE

Weigh yourself in kg and measure your height in metres. Calculate your BMI using the equation above. For example, someone weighing 60kg and 1.7 metres tall:

$$BMI = \frac{60}{1.7 \times 1.7} = 21$$

If your weight is in the acceptable range, congratulations – try and keep it there! If you are in the overweight category you should perhaps think about losing some weight but do this sensibly. You are not at greatly increased risk but weight does have a habit of creeping up gradually. If your BMI is in the 'Obese' or 'Very Obese' category you should seek medical advice on the best way to lose weight sensibly.

Before the BMI classification was developed, various tables of height and weight were available and they can still be seen, along with graphs on which an individuals height and weight can be plotted. These days most of these tables are based on the BMI system. At any one height there is a wide range of acceptable weight. This system is not concerned with fashion or what anyone wishes to look like, but with health and reduced risk of developing diet-related disease.

How common is this problem?

Around half of the adult population in Great Britain are overweight or obese and the numbers are increasing as can be seen from Figure 10 below.

Nobody knows exactly why, at a time when many people are concerned about diet and health, that the incidence of obesity and being overweight are increasing. The Health of the Nation included targets for reducing obesity but at the moment the trend is in the opposite direction.

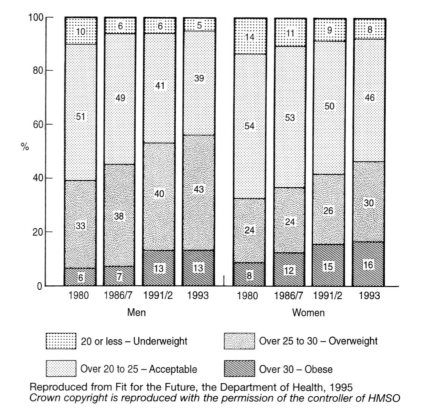

Figure 10: Proportion of men and women who fall into various weight categories (by Body Mass Index)

Why are some people overweight?

The simple answer is that people who are overweight or obese are eating more food energy (Calories) than they need. This does not mean that they are necessarily eating more or exercising less than people in the acceptable weight range. Why some people have a tendency to put on weight is not completely understood (if it were we probably would not have such a major problem!). A lot of research continues to be carried out into this problem.

What can be done?

The only way to lose weight is to eat less food energy (Calories) than when weight was increasing and to take more exercise, to use up some of the excess food energy. Losing weight and keeping weight down is very difficult. Generally, as fat in food is a concentrated source of energy, it is advisable to eat less fat by eating less high fat foods such as pastries, cakes and confectionery, and by eating low fat dairy products and lean meat. Similarly sugary foods should be reduced as they often provide food energy but little in the way of other nutrients. Starchy foods, fruit and vegetables, lean meat and low fat dairy products should form the basis of a low energy diet (see page 55).

ROLE OF NON-STARCH POLYSACCHARIDE (FIBRE) IN THE DIET

At the end of this section you should be able to
- list four medical conditions associated with lack of non-starch polysaccharide (NSP) in the diet
- explain the different effects that water soluble and insoluble fractions of NSP have on the body

In recent years the importance of eating adequate amounts of NSP has been recognised. Most people in this country do not eat enough. Low intakes of NSP can result in an increased risk of bowel disorders, like bowel cancer, diverticulosis and gallstones, as well as constipation.

The substances that make up NSP can be divided into water-soluble components (i.e. break down in water) and insoluble components. These two types of NSP have different effects on the body. The water soluble type, found mainly in fruit and vegetables and also oat bran, may help to lower blood cholesterol and possibly reduce risk of CHD. The presence of this type of NSP in the stomach also reduces the rate at which sugars are absorbed into the bloodstream – this is particularly important for diabetics (see Chapter 4).

The insoluble components give bulk to the intestines' contents and help keep the intestines healthy by making food residues move through the intestine at a reasonable speed, and thus reducing the problem of constipation.

Eating too much NSP is rarely a problem but care may be needed with young children and some elderly people.

Eating more NSP from cereals (including bread and flour), fruits and vegetables also increases the intake of starchy carbohydrates as well as a whole range of useful vitamins and minerals. Diets higher in these types of food are often lower in fat and this will help reduce the risk of CHD and becoming overweight.

SELF CHECK QUESTIONS

1   *List four dietary components that need attention if risk of certain types of cancer are to be reduced.*
2   *What proportion of the adult population are overweight or obese?*
3   *Give three reasons why we should be eating more NSP.*

WHAT CAN CATERERS DO?

By the end of this section you should be able to
- give practical suggestions as to how meals and menus can be made healthier

So far in this chapter we have looked at a range of diet-related problems that affect people in the UK. These conditions are similar, in that the type of diet recommended to help prevent them occurring is essentially the same: lower in fat, sugar and salt and higher in fibre. This is the basis of the dietary guidelines discussed in Chapter 2. Caterers are not the only group who need to be aware of dietary guidelines. Food manufacturers, retailers and the public themselves all have a responsibility.

Caterers are responsible for meals in many different types of circumstances. Implementing dietary guidelines does not mean that all meals must adhere to all guidelines all the time. Food must always look and taste good whether it is low fat or high fat! Customers will always want to treat themselves. However, there will be a need to provide customers with healthy alternatives on the menu along with information on, for example, which meals are lower in fat or low in Calories. The customers can them make their own choices.

There are a number of steps that can be taken to bring meals more in line with guidelines which do not necessarily mean rewriting all recipe books. The information given below is adapted from the Hotel, Catering and Institutional Management Association Technical Brief *Implementing Healthy Catering Practice* and the Health of the Nation *Healthy Catering Practice* (full details are in the Useful Publications list, page 198).

Recipes and ingredients

- Check recipes and reduce fat, sugar and salt levels wherever possible. Don't add sugar and salt by 'eye' as often more is added than is actually needed. Try your modified recipes out: do customers like the result? do they notice a difference? If the result is disappointing, try another version.
- Replace lard, suet, butter and pastry margarines with unsaturated margarines and white fats, together with oils such as rapeseed, sunflower, safflower, olive or nut oils. The results may taste lighter and less greasy and many people will prefer the results.
- Use a variety of both white and oily fish.
- Purchase lean cuts of meat and remove skin from poultry before cooking.

Although this may seem an expensive option there will be much less cooking loss.
◆ Use reduced fat dairy products such as semi or skimmed milk, low fat yogurt, fromage frais and low fat cheeses.
◆ Minimise the use of sweeteners such as sugar (brown and white), honey, syrup and treacle. Serve more fruit based desserts as this helps to reduce sugar levels.
◆ Use the minimum amount of salt, salty bouillons, and packet soup mixes which contain high levels of salt. Add salt after cooking and taste food before you add salt!

Cooking methods

◆ Minimise the use of deep fat frying and ensure that clean oil is used at the correct temperature to reduce absorption.
◆ Where possible bake, grill, poach, roast or steam. When grilling or roasting place food on a rack, not a tray.

Food presentation

◆ Offer alternatives together, such as butter, unsaturated and reduced fat spreads.
◆ Serve salads 'undressed' where possible and offer a range of dressings including reduced fat varieties.
◆ Fromage frais, yogurt etc. can be offered as an alternative to pouring cream for desserts. Fully skimmed milk will thicken when beaten with a high speed whisk.
◆ Bread and rolls (including wholemeal and brown varieties) should be on offer, and sandwich selections should reflect this variety. Offer a selection of high fibre biscuits and crispbreads if this is appropriate.
◆ Offer a wide variety of interesting fresh fruit, vegetables and salads; customers are becoming increasingly familiar with new foods.

Menu compilation

There can be marketing advantages to be gained from offering at least one lower fat/higher fibre/lower sugar or lower salt item in each section of your menu.

Remember, in most circumstances this is not about making your customers eat certain foods, it is about giving them the opportunity to eat more healthily if they wish!

SELF CHECK QUESTIONS

1   List four ways in which the fat content of recipes can be reduced.
2   What are the best ways to cook food to reduce the fat content?
3   List three ways in which the fibre content of meals can be increased.
4   How can you reduce the sugar content of deserts?
5   As well as actual salt, what other ingredients can add salt to a recipe?

Meeting Needs of Groups within the Population

There are various groups of people within our population who are at risk of diet-related problems. These include children, pregnant and lactating women, older people, vegetarian and some ethnic groups. This does not mean that all people within these group have 'problems' but that they are at increased risk. There are also people who need a special diet such as diabetics, coeliacs and people with food intolerance. The reasons why these groups have special nutritional needs may be the result of increased nutritional requirements, social reasons, religious and cultural beliefs or a range of medical problems.

This chapter will consider why these groups are at risk; what aspects of their diet are of concern; and the role of the caterer in meeting needs of these groups. Objectives and self-check questions are given for those groups that caterers are most likely to be providing meals for. The information given below is an introduction to these topics. The caterer will need to seek advice from an expert (e.g. a dietitian) to ensure that the meals or menus are appropriate.

CHILDREN

At the end of this section you should be able to
- explain why children have high nutritional requirements
- discuss nutritional problems common in children
- list the factors caterers should be aware of when planning school meals

Children of all ages have high requirements for all nutrients because they are growing. They are usually more active physically than adults and therefore their needs for food energy are also high. If you look at the Dietary Reference Values in Appendix 2 you will notice that despite their size, their needs for many nutrients are as high as adults. For example, boys aged 7–10 have almost the same average energy requirements as adult women, but are only likely to weigh half as much as them. Teenage children (particularly boys) have even higher requirements for energy, protein, and other nutrients.

For these high requirements to be met, children need to eat meals that are not too bulky, and are based on *The Balance of Good Food*. However, what often happens is that because they are hungry they tend to fill up on biscuits, sweets, soft drinks, chips and crisps. Although these foods can all be eaten in moderation, they shouldn't displace the more useful foods too often. The high consumption of sweet and sticky foods, often eaten between meals, is also the major cause of dental decay.

Despite children's high needs for energy and nutrients, the most widespread nutrition related problem is overweight and obesity. Although it is less common amongst children than adults there is particular concern because it may continue into adult life. Preventing obesity by eating sensibly is more likely to be successful than treating overweight in adult life; unsupervised dieting can however be dangerous in children.

Food intolerance, including food allergy, is more common in children than in adults. Fortunately, most young children will 'grow out' of this problem. More information about food intolerance is included later in this chapter (see page 68).

Iron deficiency anaemia is the most common nutritional deficiency in children. It is of particular concern in young children as they may eat a diet low in iron-containing foods. Teenage girls are also at risk due to increased requirements brought about by menstruation.

Surveys of children's eating habits suggest that in general it is teenage children, particularly girls, who are most at risk of eating diets which are low on a range of nutrients (particularly iron, but also calcium and zinc). Children from low income families are also at risk.

The role of the caterer

The main role of caterers in the provision of meals in this age group is, of course, school meals. The type of meal provided and its nutritional quality varies from school to school. Detailed nutritional guidelines are available which can help in planning meals for this age group. It is not however always straightforward: children have to eat what caterers provide. The following points should be considered:

◆ What provision is made for school meals? Where is food eaten? Who eats with whom?

◆ Are a range of meals provided that meet nutritional guidelines and take account of health, religious and ethnic preferences?

◆ How are food items priced? Do pricing policies encourage the eating of healthier options?

◆ Are 'healthier' foods presented attractively? What about tuckshop and vending machines?

◆ If appropriate continue to use beefburgers, fish fingers, chips and other children's favourites in moderation. Check that the brand you are using is not too high in fat or salt and try not to add extra fat during cooking. Serve with lower fat items.

◆ What suggestions do children have about school meals or snacks and drinks sold in school?

◆ Find out how other organisations/companies have organised meals for this age group.

SELF CHECK QUESTIONS

1   *Give two reasons why children have high nutritional requirements.*
2   *List four diet-related problems children may develop. How can caterers help?*

PREGNANT AND LACTATING WOMEN

A woman's nutritional needs increase during pregnancy and lactation to meet the needs of the developing baby and subsequently to meet the requirements of breast feeding. The diet should again be based around *The Balance of Good Health*. Additional needs should be met by satisfying the increased appetite with foods rich in essential nutrients.

OLDER PEOPLE

> At the end of this section you should be able to
> - explain the nutritional problems older people may encounter
> - list the factors important when planning meals for this age group

There are approximately 10 million people of pensionable age in this country of which up to a million are housebound. The proportion of older people in our population is increasing; by the year 2030 one in four adults will be pensioners.

The vast majority of older people live active lives, and only a relatively small proportion live in residential or nursing homes. Some older people receive Meals on Wheels, attend luncheon clubs and/or attend day centres. Many caterers are therefore involved in providing meals for this age group.

The nutritional requirements of older people do not differ greatly from those of younger adults. However as age progresses, body weight and activity decreases, and so people tend to eat less. This can result in low intakes of a range of nutrients. Their diet should be based on the dietary guidelines but with particular emphasis on **nutrient dense foods**, i.e. food rich in nutrients in a small volume of food. In addition, fruit and vegetable intakes are often low, resulting in low intakes of vitamin C and fibre. Low intakes of vitamin C can result in poor wound healing and low fibre intakes lead to constipation and bowel problems. Older people are also more at risk of a whole range of medical problems. Eating a good diet will in many instances reduce the likelihood of contracting some illnesses, and will help in recovery from many others.

The role of the caterer

Meals provided by caterers for older people should be based around *The Balance of Good Food*, with the emphasis on nutrient dense foods such as bread and cereals, meat and alternatives to meat, milk and dairy products, and fruit and vegetables. In addition the following points are important:

◆ presentation and temperature of food when served – this is particularly important for meals that are transported such as Meals on Wheels
◆ reaction of customers to the food: would you wish to eat it?
◆ are needs for special diets being met?
◆ you can try out new foods/menus; the idea that older people will only eat 'meat and two veg' does not necessarily apply
◆ can infirm older people eat it?
◆ take note of comments/suggestions made by the customers.

SELF CHECK QUESTIONS

---

1   *What type of diet should older people eat?*
2   *What is meant by the term 'nutrient dense food'?*

VEGETARIANS

At the end of this section you should be able to
- state the number of people who eat a vegetarian diet in this country
- describe the differences between a vegetarian and vegan diet
- list the important factors when designing meals or menus for vegetarians

The number of people who are **vegetarian** has risen over recent years. It is now estimated that 3–4% of adults are vegetarian and a further 10% avoid or rarely eat red meat. Vegetarianism is particularly high in young women.

Vegetarians do not eat meat; some will eat fish; most consume milk and dairy products. Their diets tend to be lower in food energy and may also be low in iron and zinc (red meat is a particularly good source of iron and zinc). On the plus side, vegetarian diets are often lower in fat, higher in fruit and vegetables and hence essential vitamins and minerals. Although the evidence is not conclusive, it appears that vegetarians have lower rates of CHD and certain cancers, although whether this is due to their diet or some other aspect of their lifestyle is not known.

A sub group of vegetarians do not eat any food of animal origin. Vegans, as they are known, can obtain all their nutrient needs from plant foods with the exception of vitamin B_{12}. However considerable care is needed to ensure that energy, protein, calcium, iron, riboflavin and vitamin D requirements are met (plant foods can be low in these nutrients).

The role of the caterer

Vegetarianism is now so widespread that on almost all menus there are meals suitable for vegetarians. They are usually highlighted in some way. They are not only eaten by vegetarians, as other people who may eat meat will often choose a vegetarian meal.

The following points should be considered when designing meals or menus for vegetarians.

◆ Provide as wide a range of foods as possible (*The Balance of Good Food* includes alternatives to meat).
◆ Try to ensure that vegetarian meals are not too high in fat (e.g. by avoiding deep fat frying and not using excessive amounts of full fat dairy products).

◆ Ensure a good mix of protein sources: cereals, pulses and nuts. This is particularly important for vegans who don't consume dairy products and rely on these foods to meet protein needs.

◆ When providing vegetarian meals for children, ensure that increased protein and energy needs are met. The use of textured vegetable protein, Quorn and similar meat replacements, and suitably fortified soya milk is recommended. For very young children ensure that the diet is not bulky and/or high in NSP. Diets high in NSP may interfere with the body's ability to absorb minerals such as iron.

SELF CHECK QUESTIONS

1   List three types of protein containing foods which vegans should eat regularly.
2   Give two reasons why particular care is necessary when planning vegetarian meals for children.

ETHNIC MINORITY GROUPS

At the end of this section you should be able to
- understand the dietary laws of the main ethnic groups living in the UK
- discuss the diet-related problems ethnic minority groups may face

A very large number of different ethnic minority groups now live in this country. The largest groups are the Asian, Afro-Caribbean and Jewish communities. Together they represent at least 5% of the UK population. Dietary practices vary greatly between different ethnic groups as well as between members of each community. The diet of the Asian and Jewish groups are affected by religious beliefs. Table 9 on page 65 highlights the dietary restrictions practised by these groups.

Within each community there are individuals who follow traditional diets more or less strictly, e.g. older people who may be socially isolated from the rest of the UK population are more likely to eat traditional foods.

In general the traditional diets of these groups provide adequate amounts of nutrients. Diets amongst Asian groups tend to be vegetarian or have low amounts of meat and/or dairy products. Recent immigrants to the UK may have difficulty in adapting their traditional diets and customs and may develop nutritional problems.

Religion	Forbidden meat	Compulsory diet	Restrictions/Strictness
Hindus	beef	Mostly vegetarian; fish rarely eaten; no alcohol	Period of fasting common
Muslim	pork	Meat must be 'Halal'; no shellfish eaten: no alcohol	Regular fasting, including Ramadan for one month
Sikhs	beef	Meat must be killed by 'one blow to the head'; no alcohol	Generally less rigid restrictions than Hindus or Muslims
Jews	pork	Meat must be 'kosher'; only fish with scales and fins eaten	Meat and dairy foods must not be consumed together

Table 9: Dietary restrictions practised by different ethnic groups

Notes: **Halal** meat is dedicated to God by a Muslim present at the killing. **Kosher** meat must be slaughtered by a Rabbinical-licensed person and then soaked and salted.

Asian vegetarian groups, particularly women and children, are at risk of low intakes of vitamin D; cases of rickets and osteomalacia have been reported. Iron deficiency anaemia can also be a problem, as the amount of iron absorbed from vegetarian and vegan traditional diets may be low.

For reasons not completely understood, Asian men and women are more at risk of CHD than the rest of the UK population. The Afro-Caribbean community is also more at risk of high blood pressure and stroke. Both communities have a higher incidence of diabetes.

The role of the caterer

People from ethnic groups may choose only to eat meals that conform to their religious and cultural beliefs. This means that they may choose not to eat in certain restaurants. However in some situations, e.g. in schools or hospitals, they may have little choice. When providing meals for people from these groups,

◆ find out as much as you about the foods/meals that are acceptable. Contact representatives of the groups, speak to religious leaders, obtain relevant recipe books; you will be surprised at the range and diversity of meals that you can provide

◆ ensure the meals and menus conform to the dietary laws; you will lose all credibility if you do not
◆ when asked about the type or source of certain ingredients give accurate information – if you don't know, say so!

SELF CHECK QUESTIONS

1   *List the main dietary laws of Hindus, Sikhs, Moslems and Jews.*
2   *Give two sources of information you should consult if you are asked to provide meals for one of these groups.*

HOSPITAL PATIENTS

By the end of this section you should be able to
- appreciate the diversity of patients for whom you may have to prepare meals
- understand that dietary guidelines used for healthy people are not always appropriate for patients

Hospital catering presents particular challenges. The typical hospital population will consist of people of all ages, with a very wide range of medical problems which may influence what they can or will eat. In general, the type of diet provided should be in line with dietary guidelines, but it must be remembered that certain individuals may need a diet higher in fat and sugar in order to increase their food energy intake. Detailed guidelines for feeding hospital patients have been published (see Useful Publications list, page 198) and should be consulted when planning menus. In addition, information will be required from the hospital dietitian, medical and nursing staff. The caterer will not be responsible for the diets of patients requiring highly specialised diets, e.g. for patients with kidney or liver problems.

The role of the caterer

◆ Ensure there is adequate choice on the menus to cover needs of the majority of patients.
◆ Be aware of the needs of children, the elderly or other at risk groups in your hospital population.
◆ Be aware of the nutritional guidelines for hospital patients and any hospital food policy.

◆ Consider special provision for certain groups:
  a   new admissions
  b   children's wards
  c   pregnant women
  d   ethnic groups
  e   vegetarians.
◆ Revise menus regularly, using information from patients about their views on the meals you provide.
◆ Ensure basic therapeutic diets can be supplied (low energy, low fat and diabetic).

DIABETICS AND COELIACS

Diabetics

Up to one million people in this country have diabetes. Diabetics have a reduced ability to control the amount of glucose in their blood. Excessively high or low levels in the blood are very serious and diet is used (along with drugs and/or insulin in some cases) to help control the condition. Because diets high in complex carbohydrates and NSP (particularly the soluble fraction) help control the rate at which sugar is absorbed into the blood, they are advised to eat a diet which has high but controlled amounts of these substances. The diet will also need to be low in sugars like sucrose, because consuming these types of carbohydrates could cause blood sugar levels to rise to dangerous levels. In practice the type of diet they should eat is similar to those recommended for other adults.

The role of the caterer

The following points are important:

◆ Most diabetics will need to eat diet high in NSP, low in sugar and fat. Caterers should be able to provide information on appropriate meals to customers who request it. Caterers have a responsibility to ensure any information is accurate.
◆ If an insulin dependent diabetic requires food immediately, some type of food must be provided. They are at risk of their blood sugar levels becoming dangerously low.
◆ Always ask for advice if you need it: in a hospital situation this should be readily available from the hospital dietitian.
◆ When preparing meals for diabetics in a hospital situation from specially designed recipes, it is extremely important that you follow the recipe accurately.

Coeliac disease

This condition is much rarer than diabetes. People with coeliac disease react to the protein gluten which is found in wheat and rye, and to a lesser extent in barley and oats. In this condition the intestinal villi through which we absorb food are lost (see Chapter 2 – Digestion and Absorption, pages 28–33). If a coeliac follows a gluten free diet they should be completely well, but they may become very ill after eating even a relatively small amount of gluten.

The role of the caterer

The following points are important when preparing a gluten free meal or diet. If you are asked which meals on your menu are suitable for a coeliac diet, make sure you give accurate information; you don't want to be responsible for making someone ill. If you aren't sure, then say so.

◆ avoid wheat, rye, barley and oats
◆ check any manufactured foods with the manufacturer. The ingredients lists on food do not have enough information to decide if it is gluten free or not
◆ use gluten free prepared foods – a wide range is available
◆ increase the NSP content of the diet by using fruit and vegetables.

FOOD INTOLERANCE

Food intolerance is a reproducible, unpleasant, non-psychological reaction to a specific food or ingredient, e.g. milk, wheat, eggs or nuts. **Food allergy** is one form of food intolerance in which there is evidence of an abnormal immunological reaction in the blood. Despite the widespread publicity surrounding intolerance to certain foods (and also additives), it is likely that only 1–2% of the population are intolerant to foods and very much less than 1% to additives. Symptoms of food intolerance include rashes, runny nose, vomiting and diarrhoea and very rarely death.

The role of the caterer

If a customer says that they are 'allergic' to a certain food or ingredient, you have a responsibility to ensure that meals are free from that specific food; although unlikely, you wouldn't want a death on your hands! This will require careful checking with suppliers. It is not always easy to tell; e.g. a milk-free diet requires a diet free from ingredients such as lactose, casein, whey hydrolysates and a range of other ingredients derived from cows milk. As with other medical conditions, if you are unsure whether or not a certain food or meal contains a certains food or ingredients, you should err on the side of caution.

EXERCISE

Plan a day's meals for one of the groups discussed in this chapter. Try to ensure that it contains all the essential nutrients as well as meeting the additional requirements of the group. If possible, discuss your ideas with someone from the relevant group. What do they think of your suggestions? Would they like to eat it? How would they improve it?

SELF CHECK QUESTIONS

1   *What type of diet should diabetics be eating?*
2   *What is coeliac disease?*
3   *Why is it important to give accurate information to customers who say they are 'allergic' to a certain food?*

Food and the Law

There are many legal requirements which govern the production and sale of food. It is beyond the scope of this text to provide a detailed examination of all of this legislation, but this chapter provides an introduction to the principal legislation in the areas of food hygiene, safety and the composition and labelling of foods.

THE FOOD SAFETY ACT 1990

By the end of this chapter you should be able to
- state the main requirements of the Food Safety Act 1990
- list the main offences and defences
- explain the role of improvement notices and prohibition orders

The main piece of legislation relating to the sale of food for human consumption is the Food Safety Act 1990. This Act updated and replaced existing legislation for England, Scotland and Wales. In other parts of the United Kingdom (Northern Ireland, the Channel Islands and the Isle of Man) similar legislation applies.

The Food Safety Act 1990 is the primary legislation in this area and most of the remaining legislation comes under its 'umbrella'. The Act provides the framework to protect customers and requires that food should not be rendered injurious to health or be contaminated in such a way that it is unfit for human consumption. It also sets out to prevent food that is not of 'the nature, substance or quality demanded' being sold, and stops food being labelled, advertised or displayed in a manner which falsely describes or misleads the customer.

In addition to this framework of customer protection measures, the Food Safety Act 1990 details enforcement powers and penalties which can be imposed if the provisions of the Act are not complied with. It is a criminal offence not to comply with this legislation.

The vast majority of the detailed requirements for food are contained in Regulations issued by Ministers. Regulations are known as secondary legislation, and are made under the umbrella of the primary legislation; in this case the Food Safety Act 1990. A wide range of Regulations exist. Some of the existing Regulations were made under previous legislation and still apply today. Others are much more recent and replace older outdated Regulations. These include the Regulations which govern specific hygiene requirements in food premises and implement the European Union (EU) Hygiene Directive (93/94 EEC): the Food Safety (General Food Hygiene) Regulations 1995. The system of secondary legislation allows specific changes to be made to minor aspects of the legislation without the need for a major review of the primary law. This has been particularly important in recent years, as there have been many changes made as a result of the implementation of EU Directives.

The main provisions of the Food Safety Act 1990

The main provisions of the Food Safety Act 1990 fall into two areas: food safety and consumer protection. As food safety can be affected by events at any point throughout the food chain, the Food Safety Act 1990 aims to control all aspects of food safety. This goes further than the more traditional 'farm gate to plate', beginning with what goes into the animals (animal feed manufacturers) or onto the crops (agricultural chemical industries).

There are four main offences concerned with food safety and consumer protection. Under the provisions of this Act, it is an offence to:

- render food injurious (harmful) to health: **Section 7**
- sell food which does not comply with food safety requirements: **Section 8**
- sell food which is not of the nature, quality or substance demanded by the consumer: **Section 14**
- falsely describe, advertise or label the product: **Section 15**

The enforcement of the Food Safety Act 1990

The Food Safety Act 1990 is enforced at a local level by the Environmental Health Officer (EHO) who is employed by the Local Authority. The EHO is the authorised officer of the enforcement authority and in this respect has powers of entry to a business and must be co-operated with. The EHO can take food or other substances for analysis and use the following powers to enforce food legislation:

Improvement notices (Section 10)

If the EHO finds that a business is failing to comply with hygiene regulations, he or she can issue an improvement notice on the proprietor of that business. This notice details the grounds for non-compliance and the measures necessary to remedy the situation. The notice also specifies a time limit (not less than 14 days) within which the specified action must be completed. A failure to comply with an improvement notice is an offence.

Prohibition order (Section 11)

If the proprietor of a food business is convicted under the Food Safety Act 1990, then a prohibition order can be issued which prevents a food business from operating. The issuing magistrate must be convinced that there is a risk to public health either from a process being used, the construction of the building or the condition of the premises within which the business operates. The prohibition order is fixed in a prominent place on the business and is valid until cancelled.

A prohibition order can also be imposed on an individual preventing them operating a food business. Only the court can lift this ban, which applies for at least six months.

Emergency prohibition order (Section 12)

If an EHO is satisfied that there is 'imminent risk to public health' then an emergency prohibition notice can be issued. The proprietor of the business concerned must be given one full day's notice of an intent to serve this notice. Within three days of serving the notice, the EHO must apply to the courts for it to be converted to an emergency prohibition order. The notice and order must be displayed conspicuously on the premises. If the application for conversion is not upheld, compensation is payable by the enforcement authority to the proprietor of the business.

Penalties and defences under the Food Safety Act 1990

A penalty of two years imprisonment and/or a fine to a maximum of £20,000 can be enforced for offences under sections 7, 8 and 14.

Section 20 provides that if the offence is due to someone other than the defendant's actions, then that other person is guilty of an offence.

Section 21 permits the defendant to prove that all reasonable precautions were taken and all due diligence exercised to prevent the offence. This defence requires that the defendant provide documentary evidence of control systems operating in the business. The **hazard analysis critical control point (HACCP)** and **Assured Safe Catering (ASC)** systems have been adopted by many businesses as control systems to provide documentary evidence which could support this defence if necessary (see Chapter 11).

REGULATIONS MADE UNDER THE FOOD SAFETY ACT 1990

It is beyond the scope of this book to examine all of the Regulations made under the Food Safety Act 1990. However, it is appropriate to consider the most recent Regulations to be implemented: the Food Safety (General Food Hygiene) Regulations 1995 and the Food Safety (Temperature Control) Regulations 1995 as these have a direct impact on all catering businesses, and the Food Labelling Regulations 1995 as these relate directly to the first part of this book.

Food Safety (General Food Hygiene) Regulations, 1995

The Food Safety (General Food Hygiene) Regulations, 1995 are designed to enforce a set of hygiene rules common to all countries within the European Union. These rules are set out in the Food Hygiene Directive (93/43 EEC). The Regulations affect anyone who sells food and anyone who works with articles that come into contact with food, e.g. refrigeration engineers, contract cleaners, etc. While these Regulations apply to all food businesses, some are also covered by more detailed Regulations specific to the products being produced, e.g. meat products manufacturers (The Meat Products (Hygiene) Regulations, 1994) and dairy product manufacturers (The Dairy Products (Hygiene) Regulations, 1995).

The Food Safety (General Food Hygiene) Regulations 1995 aim to assist employers to assess possible food safety hazards within their business and to apply appropriate controls. The emphasis of the Regulations is on the application of control measures relevant to *your* particular situation. This is because, inevitably, not all of the Regulations are equally applicable to all businesses. For example, as not all of the Regulations concerning the structure of a food premises will apply to your business, some of the requirements are followed by the words 'where appropriate' or 'where necessary'. One example concerns floor drainage, which states that *where appropriate* floors must allow surface drainage. If you have a system to ensure that water does not build up so that there is no risk to food safety, actual floor drains may not be necessary; so there is therefore no absolute requirement to have them (see *A guide to the General Food Hygiene Regulations*, Department of Health 1995).

It should be remembered that these Regulations detail the minimum hygiene standards required of food businesses. They do not specify procedures to be followed to achieve this standard, as these vary between businesses. To achieve the appropriate standards within all the different sectors of the food industry (e.g. catering, vending, food processing), the Regulations introduced the concept of voluntary industry guides to good hygiene practice.

Using a template designed to ensure that all aspects of good hygiene practice are covered, a booklet called *A Template: Industry Guides to Good Hygiene Practice* has been produced (see Useful Publications list, page 198). Using this guide, the Joint Hospitality Industry Congress has compiled a Catering Industry Guide to good hygiene practice. This details the particular legal requirements and provides guidance both on compliance and on good catering practice. You should consult this guide for further details on compliance with the Regulations in the catering industry. Details of how to obtain copies of the Template and the Catering Industry Guide are given in the Useful Publications list.

Table 10: The main requirements of the Food Safety (General Food Hygiene) Regulations 1995
Source: A Guide to the Food Safety (General Food Hygiene) Regulations 1995, Crown copyright is reproduced with the permission of the controller of HMSO

Schedule 1, Chapter 1	Equipment and Facilities	Actions
General Requirements for food premises (other than those specified in Chapter 3)		
1.1 Food Premises		Keep clean, and in good repair and condition

Schedule 1, Chapter 1 cont.	Equipment and Facilities	Actions
1.2 Layout, design, construction and size	Should permit good hygiene practices and be easy to clean and/or disinfect and should protect food against external sources of contamination such as pests	
1.3 Sanitary and hand washing facilities	Adequate facilities must be available and lavatories must not lead directly into food rooms	
1.4 Washbasins	Must have hot and cold (or mixed) running water and materials for cleaning and drying hands. **Where necessary** there must be separate facilities for washing food and food hands	Provide soap and suitable hand drying facilities
1.5 and 6 Ventilation	There must be suitable and sufficient means of natural or mechanical ventilation. Ventilation systems must be accessible for cleaning, e.g. give easy access to filters	
1.7 Lighting	Food premises must have adequate natural and/or artificial lighting	
1.8 Drainage	Adequate drainage facilities must be provided	
1.9 Changing facilities	Adequate changing facilities must be provided **where necessary**	

Schedule 1, Chapter 2	Equipment and facilities	Action
Specific requirements in rooms where foodstuffs are prepared, treated or processes (excluding dining areas and those premises specified in Chapter 3)		

Schedule 1, Chapter 2 cont.	Equipment and facilities	Action
2.1: Rooms where food is actually prepared, treated or processed	Floors, walls, ceilings and surfaces (which come into contact with food) must be adequately maintained, easy to clean and **where necessary** disinfect	Keep all surfaces, fixtures and fittings hygienic to prevent contamination of food.
2.2: Cleaning and disinfecting of tools and utensils and equipment	Provide adequate facilities, including hot and cold water, for cleaning and **where necessary** disinfecting tools and equipment	Clean and disinfect tools and equipment so as to ensure food safety
2.3: Washing of food	**Where appropriate** provide adequate facilities for washing food. Supply with hot and/ or cold water as required	Wash food properly **where necessary**

Schedule 1, Chapter 3	Equipment and facilities	Action
Requirements for movable and/or temporary premises (such as marquees, market stalls, mobile sales vehicles) premises used primarily as a private dwelling house used occasionally for catering purposes and vending machines		
3.1: Requirements for premises and vending machines	The siting, design and construction must aim to avoid contamination of food and harbouring pests	Keep clean and in good repair so as to avoid food contamination
3.2(a): Working practices movable or temporary premises	Provide appropriate facilities for personal hygiene	Take all reasonable, practical steps to avoid the risk of contamination of food or ingredients
3.2(b): Surfaces	Surfaces in contact with food must be easy to clean and **where necessary** to disinfect	Take all reasonable, practical steps to avoid the risk of contamination of food or ingredients

Schedule 1, Chapter 3 cont.	Equipment and facilities	Action
3.2(c) & (d): Cleaning of utensils and foodstuffs	Adequate provision must be made for cleaning of foodstuffs and the cleaning and where necessary the disinfection of utensils and equipment	Take all reasonable, practical steps to avoid the risk of contamination of food or ingredients
3.2(e): Hot and cold water supply	An adequate supply of hot and/or cold potable water must be available	Take all reasonable, practical steps to avoid the risk of contamination of food or ingredients
3.2(f): Waste storage and disposal	Adequate arrangements for the storage and disposal of waste	Take all reasonable, particle steps to avoid the risk of contamination of food or ingredients

Schedule 1, Chapter 4 Transport	Equipment and facilities	Action
4.1: Containers and vehicles for the transport of food	**Where necessary** their design must allow them to be adequately cleaned and disinfected	Keep clean and in good order to prevent contamination
4.2: Dedicated containers and vehicles used for bulk transport of food in liquid, granular, or powder form	Containers or vehicles used must be reserved for food only and marked as such, when there is a risk of contamination	Do not use containers or vehicles to transport anything other than food where this may result in contamination
4.3: Containers or vehicles used for different food or both foods and non-foods		**Where necessary** separate different products effectively to protect against the risk of contamination
4.4: Where different products have been carried in the same containers		Effectively clean them between loads to avoid the risk of contamination

Schedule 1, Chapter 4 Transport cont.	Equipment and facilities	Action
4.5 Minimising the risk of contamination		Foodstuffs in conveyances or containers must be placed so as to minimise the risk of contamination

Schedule 1, Chapter 5 Equipment and requirements	Equipment and facilities	Action
5.1: Equipment requirements	Articles, fittings and equipment that can come into contact with food shall be made of materials and maintained so that they, and the surrounding areas, can be kept clean, and **where necessary**, disinfected	All equipment and surfaces that come into contact with food must be kept clean

Schedule 1, Chapter 6 Food Waste	Equipment and facilities	Action
6.1: Food and other waste		Do not allow food and other waste to gather in food rooms, unless this is unavoidable for the proper functioning of your food business
6.2: Containers for food and other waste	Containers must be able to be closed unless the environmental health services are satisfied that this is not appropriate. They must be kept in good condition and **where necessary** be easy to clean and disinfect	

Schedule 1, Chapter 6 Food Waste cont.	Equipment and facilities	Action
6.3: Arrangements for the storage and removal of waste	Refuse stores should be designed and constructed to be easily cleaned and prevent pests gaining access	Arrange for the proper periodic removal of the refuse and keep the area clean, and protect against pests and contamination

Schedule 1, Chapter 7 Water supply	Equipment and facilities	Action
7.1: Water supply	There must be an adequate supply of potable (drinking) water	**Where necessary**, for food safety, use potable water to prevent contamination
7.2: Ice		**Where appropriate**, ice must be made from potable water to prevent contamination. Ice should be stored and handled carefully to protect it from contamination

Schedule 1, Chapter 8 Personal hygiene	Equipment and facilities	Action
8.1: Personal hygiene	Food handlers must wear suitable clean, and **where appropriate, protective clothing**	Everyone in a food handling area must maintain a high level of personal cleanliness
8.2: Infected food handlers		No one suffering from a disease which could be transmitted through food should work in a food handling area

Schedule 1, Chapter 9 Provision applicable to foodstuffs	Equipment and facilities	Action
9.1: Raw materials		No raw materials or ingredients should be accepted if known or suspected of being contaminated and which would still be unfit after normal sorting or processing
9.2: Protection of raw materials from contamination		At any stage of the business operation food must be protected from contamination likely to render it unfit for human consumption

Schedule 1, Chapter 10 Training	Equipment and facilities	Action
10.1: Training		All food handlers must be supervised and instructed and/or trained in food hygiene matters to a level appropriate to their job

Food Safety (Temperature Control) Regulations 1995

These Regulations stipulate that 'No person shall keep raw materials, ingredients, intermediate products, and finished products likely to support the growth of pathogenic micro-organisms, or the formation of toxins at temperatures which would result in a risk to health.'

They require foods which could support the growth of pathogenic (disease-causing) micro-organisms or the formation of toxins to be held at temperatures less than 8°C or greater than 63°C. Unlike the Regulations they replace, the Food Safety (Temperature Control) Regulations 1995 do not list specific foods which must be kept under temperature controlled conditions, as this is left to the managers of food businesses. There is tolerance within the Regulations to allow for a temperature rise which would be consistent with food preparation and/or processing.

The types of food which must be held at temperatures less than 8°C are those often described as **high-risk foods**. This term is used to identify foods which, given the right conditions, would be very likely to support the growth of pathogenic micro-organisms and/or the production of toxins. The conditions necessary for a high-risk food to support microbial growth would include a failure to store the product at low temperatures. High risk foods include:

◆ dairy products, including milk, soft cheeses and dairy based desserts
◆ cooked items which contain meat, fish, eggs or cheese
◆ smoked and cured fish and meats
◆ partly cooked pastry and dough products.

It should be remembered that many bacteria, including some **pathogens** can grow at temperatures of less than 8°C. Whilst the majority of these bacteria grow slowly, some, such as *Listeria monocytogenes,* can grow at temperatures as low as 1°C and it may therefore be more appropriate to store some foods at temperatures well below the 8°C limit.

Foods which have been reheated or cooked and are to be sold hot must be held at temperatures greater than 63°C. This is to prevent the growth of surviving organisms, the germination of any surviving spores or toxin production. Foods should not be held hot for longer than two hours and should subsequently be cooled rapidly to less than 8°C, or discarded.

For further details, see the Regulations themselves (HMSO Publications) and the *Guidance on the Food Safety (Temperature Control) Regulations 1995* published by the Department of Health.

Food Labelling Regulations 1995 (Draft)

Food labels are required to carry certain information by law. Most food labels must give:

◆ name of the food
◆ list of ingredients
◆ Use-By or Best Before information
◆ any special storage conditions or conditions of use (e.g. store in a refrigerator)
◆ name and address
◆ place of origin (if appropriate)
◆ instructions for use (if appropriate)
◆ weight

This information must be on most food sold to consumers and to caterers.

A food can't claim to be 'reduced calorie' unless it is much lower in calories than the usual version.

When a product makes claims like these, it should back it up by giving the minimum amount either here where the claim is made or in the ingredients list.

Ingredients, including additives, are listed in descending order of weight at the time of their use in the preparation of the food. We can use the list to compare products for value, or to avoid ingredients we don't like.

Most additives must be listed, saying what their job is. The food company can use the name or the number (if the additive has been given one in the UK, with an 'E' if also agreed by the European Community). Both can be given.

If flavourings are used the packet must say, or give the names of each one. *They* don't have numbers.

This is where we can check what 'reduced calorie' amounts to. More companies are giving this information even if not making a claim.

Datemark must appear on the product.

Instructions for safe storage.

Name and address of the maker, packer or retailer, so we can write to them if we want.

The big e means that the average quantity must be accurate, but the weight of each pack may vary slightly.

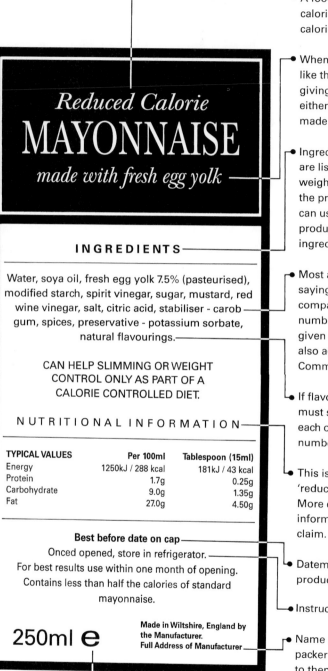

Reduced Calorie
MAYONNAISE
made with fresh egg yolk

INGREDIENTS

Water, soya oil, fresh egg yolk 7.5% (pasteurised), modified starch, spirit vinegar, sugar, mustard, red wine vinegar, salt, citric acid, stabiliser - carob gum, spices, preservative - potassium sorbate, natural flavourings.

CAN HELP SLIMMING OR WEIGHT CONTROL ONLY AS PART OF A CALORIE CONTROLLED DIET.

NUTRITIONAL INFORMATION

TYPICAL VALUES	Per 100ml	Tablespoon (15ml)
Energy	1250kJ / 288 kcal	181kJ / 43 kcal
Protein	1.7g	0.25g
Carbohydrate	9.0g	1.35g
Fat	27.0g	4.50g

Best before date on cap
Onced opened, store in refrigerator.
For best results use within one month of opening.
Contains less than half the calories of standard mayonnaise.

250ml e

Made in Wiltshire, England by the Manufacturer.
Full Address of Manufacturer

Figure 11: Food label giving information which is required by law
Source: Food Sense, Understanding Food Labels
Reproduced with permission of the Department of Health

The typical label in Figure 11 on page 82 shows how most of this information can be displayed.

Labels are useful for the following reasons. They help us choose food we like or require; they give us the freedom to avoid ingredients we do not want or should not eat, such as certain foods or additives; they help in avoiding food poisoning. Most food have the Use-By or Best Before date on them. The Use-By date mark is for highly perishable foods which could become a food safety risk. Foods must not be kept or eaten beyond this date. The Best Before date is usually on found on foods that can be kept longer. If food is kept after this date it may not be dangerous but it will not be at its best. However, most foods start to deteriorate eventually.

Many food labels also include information about the nutritional content of the food. Food companies do not have to give this information, but if they decide to do so or make a nutritional claim on a product, the information must be given in one of the following two formats.

Energy (kJ and kcal)	OR	Energy (kJ and kcal)
Protein (g)		Protein (g)
Carbohydrate (g)		Carbohydrate (g)
Fat(g)		of which sugars (g)
		Fat(g)
		of which saturates (g)
		Fibre (g)
		Sodium(g)

All information must be given per 100g or per 100 ml of food.

The EU Directive (90/496/EEC) contains the relevant legislation on nutrition labelling. For more information about food labelling see the Food Sense leaflets, *Understanding Food Labels* and *About Food Additives*.

The impact of EU legislation

Since joining the Common Market in 1972, the UK Government has made many hundreds of Regulations to ensure compliance with EU (European Union) Directives. In addition to the Directives which are not directly binding on member states, the EU can implement its own legally binding Regulations. These regulations do not require member states to create legislation to implement them, as they are binding in themselves. Contraventions of EU Regulations are considered in the European Court. The EU also makes

Recommendations which are not binding but which are expected to influence the policy development in member states.

OTHER LEGISLATION (HSAWA, COSHH)

In addition to the Food Safety Act 1990, other legislation governs specific aspects of food production and safety. Specific sectors of the food industry, such as the meat and dairy sectors, are governed by particular Regulations, and food related illnesses and infectious diseases are governed by Public Health legislation. In addition, legislation governs our health and safety at work.

The Health and Safety at Work Act 1974 applies both to employees and to the general public. It sets out to create an awareness of the need for high standards of health and safety at work and requires employers to prepare and implement a safety policy. The Control of Substances Hazardous to Health Regulations 1994 (COSHH) form part of this awareness to safety and are considered below with particular reference to cleaning and disinfection.

The Control of Substances Hazardous to Health Regulations 1994

Within the scope of these Regulations, substances hazardous to health are defined as those chemicals labelled by the manufacturers as being toxic, irritant, harmful or corrosive.

It is the legal responsibility of employers to assess all operations within a business which are likely to expose an employee to substances classed as being harmful to health. The assessment evaluates the risk to health and then identifies the measures necessary to minimise those risks. The employer must provide all the necessary equipment to protect the employee whilst using the substance concerned. The final part of the COSHH assessment demands that employees should be trained in the use of equipment as appropriate, and instructed in the need for care and the appropriate measures should an accident occur.

The COSHH Regulations cover the cleaning chemicals and disinfectants used in catering. The manufacturers of these chemicals are required to provide information about the hazards associated with the chemical they sell, but the evaluation of a chemical's safety as it is used in your business must be undertaken by you, in your premises. Finally, remember that if you change a cleaning agent or a disinfectant, the COSHH assessment for the replacement product, appropriate safety information and necessary safety equipment must be in place **before** you start to use the chemical.

It is important that you become familiar with all those aspects of the law which affect you at work. This is your responsibility and 'ignorance is no defence'. Several useful texts are listed in the Useful Publications list on page 198.

Food Hygiene and Microbiology

This chapter examines the relationship between food hygiene and microbiology. It introduces you to the different types of micro-organisms which exist and to those found in food. The main sources of micro-organisms are described and the main routes by which our food is contaminated are outlined.

THE RELATIONSHIP BETWEEN FOOD HYGIENE AND MICROBIOLOGY

Food hygiene is the means by which we ensure the safety of the food we prepare and eat. This includes the ways in which we protect food from contamination by:

◆ micro-organisms (e.g. salmonella) or their toxins (poisons: e.g. botulinum toxin)
◆ pests e.g. flies or rodents
◆ foreign bodies e.g. nails, glass or plastic
◆ chemicals e.g. pesticides or cleaning fluids.

The ways in which you prepare and store food must also reduce the risk of food contamination so that your customers are not at risk of illness or injury. Similarly, the process of cleaning food preparation areas should be such that any risk of food contamination by harmful chemicals is minimised. As you can see, food hygiene incorporates all aspects of food preparation from the point at which the raw materials are received from suppliers, through to the point of sale or consumption of the finished product.

In order that you handle food in a safe and hygienic manner, it is necessary to learn about the various aspects of food hygiene. This includes learning about micro-organisms and their association with both our food and the food preparation environment (e.g. a kitchen). You must also learn about the different chemicals used to clean and disinfect the food preparation environment. You need to be able to recognise the pests which may find their way into a kitchen and know how to get rid of them safely. Perhaps more importantly, you need to understand how the structure and layout of a catering operation can prevent an infestation in the first place. Finally you need to understand the relationship between the people who handle food (you) and food poisoning and contamination, so that you can prevent incidents such as those described in the headlines below.

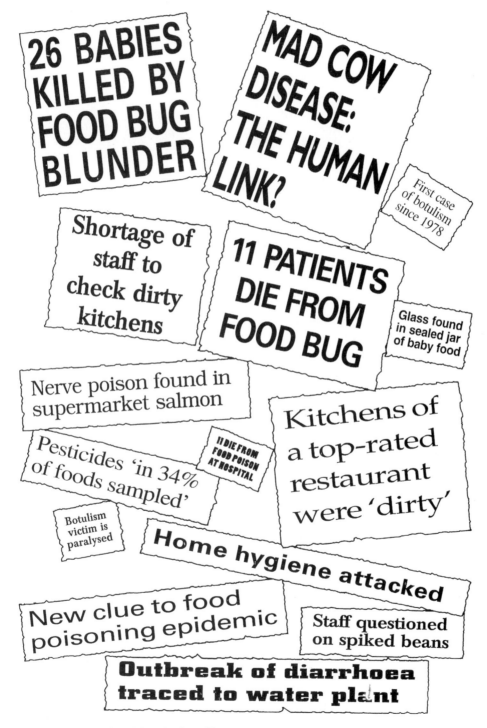

Figure 12: Food safety hits the headlines

This section of this book will examine the various aspects of food microbiology and hygiene and, through a range of exercises, will show how food hygiene can be managed.

BASICS OF FOOD MICROBIOLOGY

By the end of this section you will be able to:
- identify the main groups of micro-organisms
- describe how moulds, yeasts and bacteria reproduce

Microbiology is the study of micro-organisms. Food microbiology is the study of micro-organisms and their relationship to our food. Some types of micro-organisms are beneficial and are used extensively in food production, but other types are responsible for many undesirable effects in food. If present in food in large enough numbers, some bacteria cause illness (food poisoning). Microbes can also cause food spoilage, e.g. the souring of milk, the growth of moulds on foods such as bread and cheese. A knowledge of the nature of micro-organisms, their growth requirements, and how growth can be prevented, is essential if you are to understand correct procedures of hygiene, as well as the principles involved in the various methods of food preservation.

How big are micro-organisms?

'Micro-organism' means very small organism. The size of micro-organisms is usually measured in micrometers (μm). A micrometer is one 1000th of a millimetre or one 1 000 000th of a metre. The diagram below shows the size relationships of some micro-organisms.

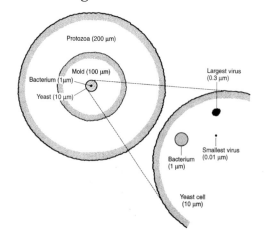

Figure 13: The size relationships between micro-organisms

Biological groupings of micro-organisms

Micro-organisms can be grouped into five biological types:

1   Protozoa

2   Algae

3   Viruses

4   Microscopic fungi – moulds and yeasts

5   Bacteria

Protozoa

Protozoa are small single-celled animals. They are capable of independent movement. They mostly live in water, e.g. in ponds, rivers, the sea and in the water in soil. A common example is *Amoeba*.

Protozoa feed by engulfing tiny food particles and reproduce by binary fission, i.e. dividing into two. The majority of protozoa are **non-pathogenic** (do not cause disease), but there are a few **pathogenic** (disease causing) species. For example, *Entamoeba histolytica* causes amoebic dysentery, common in tropical countries. *Toxoplasma gondii* is an organism sometimes found in animals (particularly cats) which may be transmitted to man during the handling of raw meat (particularly pork and mutton). The disease known as toxoplasmosis, has recently become of more concern in this country.

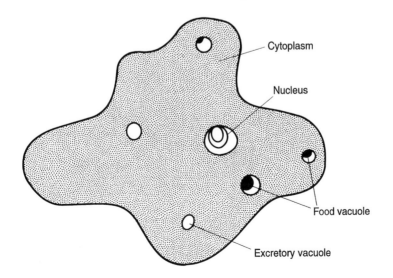

Figure 14: A diagrammatic representation of a protozoan

Algae

Algae are simple plants. Some are visible with the naked eye (e.g. seaweeds), but many are microscopic. They contain the green pigment chlorophyll or a similar pigment which enables them to photosynthesise. This means that they do not require complex organic substances but can utilise carbon dioxide from the air and water to make food. Microscopic algae usually live in water. Although each cell can survive on its own, they tend to grow in a mass and are often visible as green slime on the surface of ponds. Some types of algae (such as chlorella) can be grown on the surface of water, harvested, and used as a source of protein.

1 Virus lands on the surface of the cell and attaches to the membrane

2 The membrane of the virus integrates with that of the cell it is infecting (the host cell)

3 The viral genome enters the host cell and migrates to the nucleus where it merges with the genetic material of the host cell

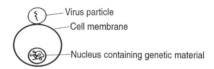

4 The presence of the viral genome makes the host cell start replicating the component parts of new virus particles

5 These are assembled into new viruses – this process repeats until the host cell is full

6 The host cell bursts (and dies) releasing many millions of new copies of the virus

Figure 15: How a virus particle replicates

Viruses

These are the smallest of all micro-organisms, varying in size from 0.01–0.3µm. Unlike other micro-organisms viruses do not have a cellular structure. They are particles made up of a central core of **nucleic acid** (usually **DNA** but sometimes **RNA**) surrounded by a protein coat. They cannot feed, grow or multiply in isolation. They can only survive as **parasites** in larger living cells. To replicate, a virus particle attaches itself to a cell and the core of the virus penetrates its **nucleus**. The nucleic acid from the virus combines with that of the cell and directs it to produce more virus particles (see Figure 15). These new particles are then set free to attack other cells. The cell that was attacked first (the host cell) is injured or even destroyed by the invading virus, therefore viruses are always **pathogenic**, i.e. they cause disease in their hosts.

Host	Viral Disease
Man	Common cold, Mumps, Measles Chicken pox, Hepatitis A, Polio
Animals	Foot and Mouth Disease, Rabies, Distemper
Plants	Mosiac Diseases, Rusts

Table 11: Some common viral diseases

Most viral diseases in man are transmitted by contact, but some are known to be transmitted by contaminated food or water, e.g. hepatitis A and poliomyelitis. Thousands of pounds are lost annually due to destruction of crops and livestock by virus diseases (see Table 11).

Microscopic Fungi

Unlike green plants, the fungi do not possess any chlorophyll. They are, therefore, unable to photosynthesise and require complex **organic** compounds as food. Those that grow and feed on dead organic material are termed **saprophytes**, while those feeding on living plants and animals are **parasites**. Some fungi are visible to the naked eye, e.g. mushrooms. Others are microscopic, and these fungi are divided into two groups, the moulds and the yeasts.

Moulds

Moulds are usually multicellular, i.e. each mould consists of more than one cell. However, each cell is capable of independent growth and moulds may therefore be classified as micro-organisms.

Reproduction in moulds is chiefly by means of **asexual** spores. In some moulds the spores are formed within a spore case or **sporanguim** at the tip of a **fertile** or **aerial hypha** (plural: **hyphae**). Other moulds reproduce by forming unprotected spores known as **conidia**. These are cut off, either singly or in chains, from the tip of a fertile hypha (see Figure 16). These mechanisms are used to classify moulds. When ripe, the spores are released into the air. If they find their way to a suitable **substrate** (food) they germinate and produce a new growth of mould. Some moulds also produce sexual spores by the fusion of two hyphae.

Many moulds cause food spoilage, which can even occur in refrigerated foods. However, certain moulds are used in food production, particularly in cheese-making. Danish Blue, Roquefort and Camembert are mould ripened.

Although most moulds are harmless, a few are pathogenic and cause diseases in plants, such as potato blight and skin infections in humans, such as athlete's foot and ringworm. Certain moulds are capable of causing illness by producing poisons or toxins in foods known as mycotoxins. The mould *Aspergillus flavus* produces aflatoxin. This has been found in groundnuts (peanuts), figs and cereals. High levels of aflatoxin are associated with cancer of the liver. Ergot is a fungus which attacks rye and it can cause a serious, sometimes fatal illness (ergotism) in people who eat bread made from infected grain. This illness, known as St Anthony's Fire, was very common in the Middle Ages.

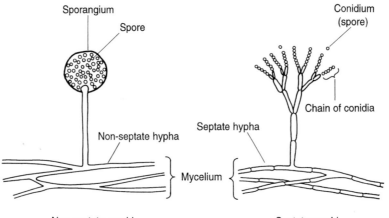

Figure 16: The structure of some common moulds

Yeasts

Yeasts are simple single-celled fungi. They are mainly **saprophytic** and usually grow on plant foods. Yeast cells may be oval, rod shaped or spherical. They are larger than bacteria and under a high power microscope a distinct nucleus is visible.

Most yeasts reproduce asexually, by a simple process known as **budding**. In one part of the cell the cytoplasm bulges out of the cell wall. This bud grows in size and finally separates as a new yeast cell (see Figure 17).

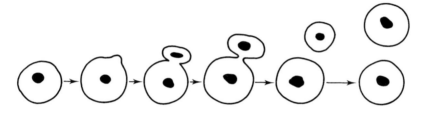

Figure 17: Budding – asexual reproduction in yeasts

Yeasts may cause spoilage in certain foods, e.g. fruit juices, jams and meat. These yeasts are normally referred to as wild yeasts in order to distinguish them from those used commercially in the production of alcoholic drinks and bread.

The economic importance of yeast lies in its ability to break down carbohydrate foods into alcohol and carbon dioxide. This process, known as alcoholic fermentation, is **anaerobic**, i.e. takes place in the absence of oxygen. Yeast contains the **enzyme** zymase, which is responsible for the fermentation of sugars, such as glucose into ethanol (alcohol) and carbon dioxide.

$$C_6H_{12}O_6 \longrightarrow 2C_2H_5OH + 2CO_2$$

Glucose   **Zymase**   Ethanol   Carbon dioxide

This is an incomplete reaction, and if a plentiful supply of oxygen is available, yeast cells will respire aerobically. In this case, yeast enzymes are able to break down sugars more completely and carbon dioxide and water are produced.

$$C_6H_{12}O_6 + 6O_2 \longrightarrow 6CO_2 + 6H_2O$$

Glucose   Oxygen   Carbon Dioxide   Water

Bacteria

Bacteria are widely distributed in the environment. They are found in air, water and soil; in the intestines of animals; on the moist linings of our mouths, noses and throat; and on the surface of our body and on plants. Bacteria are the smallest single-celled micro-organisms, some being only 0.4µm in diameter. The cell contains a mass of cytoplasm and some nuclear material (DNA). Unlike mould and yeast cells the bacterial cell does not have a distinct nucleus. The cell is enclosed by a rigid cell wall (as in plants) and in some bacteria this is surrounded by a **capsule** or slime layer. The capsule consists of a mixture of a mixture of polysaccharides and polypeptides. Inside the cell wall is the flexible cell membrane (also known as the plasma membrane); this controls the passage of nutrients into the cell and the movement of waste out of the cell. Within the plasma membrane, the cell contents are suspended in the cytoplasm.

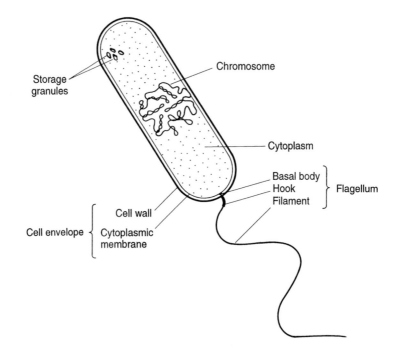

Figure 18: The structure of a bacterial cell

Bacteria can be classified into groups, depending on the shape of the cells:

1   Coccus (plural: cocci) – spherical.

(a)   (b)

Figure 19: Cocci
(a) Staphylococcus (Boils and food poisoning)
(b) Streptococcus (Tonsillitis)

2   Bacillus (plural: bacilli) – rod shaped.

Figure 20: Bacilli

3   Vibrio – short curved rods.

Figure 21: Vibrio

Some bacteria are capable of independent movement. These bacteria possess long thread like structures called **flagella**, which originate from inside the cell membrane. The flagella move in a whip-like manner and help to propel the bacteria through liquid.

Bacteria reproduce by a process known as **binary fission**. The nuclear material reproduces itself and divides into two separate parts and then the rest of the cell divides producing two daughter cells, which are equal in size. The time taken to do this is called the **generation time**. Given optimum growing conditions, some bacteria can divide in as little as 10 minutes, although it usually takes around 20 minutes.

Because bacteria often multiply rapidly to such large numbers, they often run short of food. In such cases most bacteria die, but there are some bacteria which

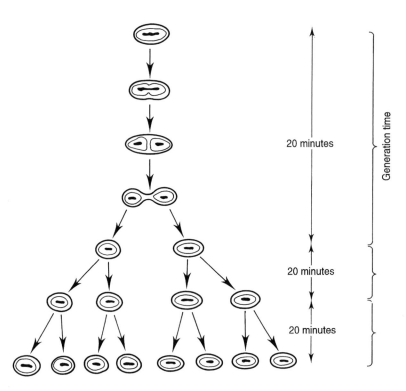

Figure 22: Binary fission in bacteria

can produce **spores** or **endospores** (usually referred to as spores) which enable them to survive.

Spores are hard, resistant bodies, which are formed by some types of bacteria when they are unable to obtain the materials necessary for growth and survival in the environment. The spore is formed within the bacterial cell; the rest of the cell then disintegrates, releasing the preformed spore. Unlike mould spores, bacterial spores are dormant non-reproductive forms of the cell. They are designed to survive in this form until conditions become favourable for growth (see Figure 23, page 97).

Spores can survive unfavourable conditions for very long periods of time. When conditions become favourable, the spore germinates, producing a new bacterial cell. Spore formation occurs in only certain **genera** of bacteria: *Bacillus* and *Clostridium* are both spore forming bacteria found in food. Because bacterial spores are resistant to heat, they can survive in food when it is cooked. They are also resistant to cold (e.g. refrigeration and freezing) and to many chemical products designed to kill bacteria, such as disinfectants.

Having examined the different types of micro-organisms which exist, it should be noted that this text concentrates on bacterial interactions in food, as these

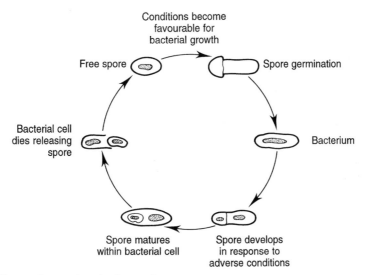

Figure 23: Spore formation in bacteria

are the most important. There will be some discussion of the role of the fungi, particularly in food spoilage and limited mention of viruses and protozoa (food poisoning).

SELF CHECK QUESTIONS

1   How do moulds and yeasts reproduce?
2   How do bacteria reproduce?
3   Why do bacteria produce spores?

SOURCES OF MICRO-ORGANISMS IN OUR FOOD

By the end of this section you will be able to
- describe the main routes of microbial food contamination
- list the main sources of micro-organisms in our food
- list the main mechanisms which can prevent microbial contamination of foods

---

EXERCISE

Before you read this section, complete the following exercise. If there are things you are not sure about you can fill in the gaps after reading this section.

In the centre of a large sheet of blank paper draw a carrot (to represent vegetable foods) and a cow (to represent animal foods). Now, using a series of words and arrows, identify the major sources of micro-organisms in our foods and the main routes of contamination. For example, the soil is a major source of micro-organisms which contaminate plants, so draw (or write) soil and draw an arrow which goes from the soil to the carrot. Animal feeds are a possible source of micro-organisms which contaminate animals, so draw a sack of animal feed and draw an arrow from that to the cow. You will end up with a chart of inter connecting routes of contamination routes. Once you have done this, read the following section and fill in any gaps in your chart.

Micro-organisms occur everywhere in the natural environment, thus all living and dead plants and animals have micro-organisms associated with, on and in them. These are the micro-organisms naturally associated with the foods we eat.

The main sources of micro-organisms in our food are:

- soil and water
- plants and plant products
- animals
- air
- food utensils and equipment
- food handlers.

Soil and water

Soil contains the greatest variety of micro-organisms. The drying of the surface of soils caused by wind gives rise to dust particles which contain micro-organisms. These particles are then carried by the wind. The formation of clouds and then rain washes this dust from the sky, depositing the micro-organisms in the dust particles back onto the ground. Of the micro-organisms important in food microbiology many moulds, yeasts and bacteria of the **genera** *Bacillus, Clostridium, Escherichia, Pseudomonas* and *Streptococcus* are all found in the soil.

Natural waters such rivers, lakes and streams contain not only their own specific range of micro-organisms but also those from the soil washed in by surface waters. The number of bacteria in water varies depending on the source of the water. For example, stream water which contains run-off from a field in which cows have been grazing, is likely to contain **faecal** organisms and other organisms from the animal. The main types of bacteria likely to be found in water are *Pseudomonas*, *Proteus*, *Micrococcus*, *Bacillus*, *Streptococcus* and *Escherichia*. The last two genera are likely **faecal** contaminants of water.

Plants and plant products

Soil and water are the main source of micro-organisms found on plants. Other organisms found on plants depend upon the type of plant and the environment in which it is grown. Plants frequently carry bacteria of the genera *Pseudomonas*, *Micrococcus*, *Lactobacillus*, *Listeria*, *Streptococcus* and *Bacillus*, including the potential pathogens *Listeria monocytogenes* and *Bacillus cereus*. Among the moulds most likely to be present are those responsible for the spoilage of plant products, especially fruits, after harvest. These micro-organisms are responsible for the so-called **market diseases**. This is a general term used to describe a group of diseases which are responsible for the loss of approximately 20% of all fruit and vegetables harvested for human consumption.

Animals

Sources of micro-organisms from animals include those on the outside (the skin) and the inside (within the respiratory tract and the gastrointestinal tract). The micro-organisms from the inside of the animal usually cause the most problems. However, hides, hoofs, hair and feathers do contain large numbers of organisms from soil, manure, feed and water. The skin of many meat animals is also a source of *Staphylococcus aureus* and from this source the organisms may find their way onto the carcass meat. Similarly the faeces of many carcass animals is a source of *Salmonella*, which may cause the animal no harm but could cause disease in humans.

All animals return their waste (and the micro-organisms within it) to the soil and water and thus eventually to the plants growing there. This mechanism is increasingly recognised as an important route in the transmission of potential **pathogens** to our food crops, particularly if animal manure is used as a fertiliser.

Food utensils and equipment

The types of micro-organisms associated with food equipment depend upon the types of food which comes into contact with the equipment and how the equipment has been cleaned. Utensils such as bowls and knives, which may be used for both raw and cooked foods in the day-to-day operation of a kitchen, must be cleaned thoroughly to prevent them becoming a vehicle for the transfer of micro-organisms.

Food handlers

The numbers and types of micro-organisms found on food handlers' outer garments vary, depending upon how often the clothes are changed. The population would normally consist of organisms associated with items handled by the individual. It is also likely that organisms from the skin, including *Staphylococcus aureus*, would be present. Faecal organisms present on outer clothing may indicate poor personal hygiene. See Chapter 9 for more details of the food handler's role in carrying micro-organisms.

CONTAMINATION OF FOOD WITH UNWANTED MICRO-ORGANISMS

EXERCISE

Before you read the following section:

1   Take the chart you completed earlier and using a coloured pen put a bar across each arrow at a point where contamination could be prevented.

2   Identify the means by which contamination could be prevented at the points you have identified.

You have seen how food can be contaminated with a wide range of micro-organisms from a variety of sources. Whilst most of these organisms are unlikely to cause us harm, some are **pathogenic**. It is impossible to expect raw, untreated foods to be free from micro-organisms, but it is not unreasonable to expect pathogens to be absent or present in very low numbers. This can be achieved in a number of ways, including:

◆ the heat treatment of animal foodstuffs
◆ restricted access to grazing land treated with sewage fertilisers
◆ controlled use of antibiotics to prevent illness amongst livestock
◆ veterinary inspections at the point of slaughter to prevent sick animals being slaughtered for human food
◆ high standards of hygiene and animal husbandry
◆ appropriate storage of raw foods prior to and during processing and preparation.

EXERCISE

You may have identified some specific examples of these factors when you completed the exercise for this section. Go back to your diagram (see page 98) and see where these mechanisms fit in.

SELF-CHECK QUESTIONS

---

1   *What are the main sources of micro-organisms in our food?*
2   *Describe how faecal organisms may get into our food.*

7

Controlling Micro-organisms in our Food

In the previous chapter you have been introduced to the different groups of micro-organisms and have learned how they get into our food. The presence of micro-organisms in our food eventually causes it to spoil and become unfit to eat. The time this takes in raw foods can be increased by manipulating storage conditions. This is because micro-organisms need specific environmental conditions to enable them to grow. Food manufacturers and food processors selectively manipulate these conditions to prevent or minimise microbial growth: this is called food preservation. In this chapter you will learn about the factors that affect the growth of micro-organisms, and then you will examine them in relation to food spoilage and preservation.

FACTORS AFFECTING THE GROWTH OF MICRO-ORGANISMS

By the end of this section you will be able to
- list the factors that affect the growth of micro-organisms
- describe how these factors affect the growth of bacteria

All micro-organisms require certain environmental conditions for growth and multiplication. We shall consider these factors with particular reference to bacteria, but don't forget however that ALL micro-organisms are affected by these growth constraints.

Time

The rate of multiplication of bacteria varies according to the species and to the conditions of growth. Under optimum conditions (which are different for each organism) most bacteria reproduce by **binary fission** once every 20 minutes, producing several million cells in under seven hours. The time it takes bacteria to divide is called the **generation time**.

Fortunately, growth does not carry on at such a rapid rate for any great length of time. The life cycle of a **bacterial colony** has been investigated and it has been found that when bacteria are placed on a fresh growth medium there is no multiplication for about 30 minutes. This is called the **lag phase**. During this time the cells are **metabolising** rapidly, but this activity results in a slight increase in cell size, rather than in cell numbers. Following this, the cells multiply rapidly for a few hours – the **log phase** – so called because growth is **logarithmic**. The colony then enters a **stationary phase** of growth where the number of cells produced is equal to the number of cells dying. Finally, the growth rate decreases, usually due to a combination of factors including a shortage of food and an increase in the concentration bacterial waste products. This is called the **decline phase**.

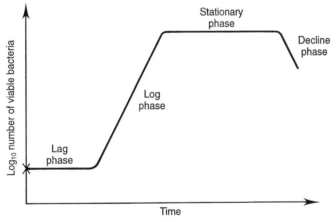

Figure 24: The bacterial growth curve

Food

There are two basic types of nutrition:

1   **Autotrophic nutrition**   Autotrophic organisms resemble plants since they are able to use chemically simple inorganic substances as food. Many bacteria are autotrophic and there are relatively few substances that are not bio-degradable, i.e. that cannot be broken down by a species of bacteria.

2   **Heterotrophic nutrition**   Heterotrophic organisms resemble animals since they require chemically complex organic substances such as protein and carbohydrate for food. All moulds and yeasts and some bacteria, including most **pathogens** and all the bacteria you will learn about in this book, are heterotrophic.

All heterotrophic micro-organisms require nutrients which will supply the following:

◆ energy: obtained from carbon containing substances (usually carbohydrates but fats and alcohol can be used)
◆ nitrogen for protein synthesis
◆ vitamins
◆ minerals.

Moisture

Micro-organisms, like all other organisms, require water to maintain life. The exact amount of water required varies. Whilst micro-organisms cannot grow in dried foods products such as flour, mould spores may survive. This can be a problem if the product gets damp, as the spores can then germinate and the product can rapidly become mouldy. Bacterial spores can also survive in dried products, but because bacteria need more moisture to grow than moulds, the products are not likely to be spoiled by bacteria unless they get very wet.

The amount of water that is available in a food for micro-organisms to use can be described in terms of the **water activity (a_w)**. Pure water has an a_w = 1.0 (i.e. 100% of the water is available for micro-organisms to use). The water activity of most fresh foods is more than 0.98 (98% of water available for micro-organisms to use) but dissolved substances, such as sugar and salt, may lower this; e.g. a saturated salt solution has an a_w = 0.75 (75% of water is available). Bacteria normally require more available moisture than yeasts and moulds.

The addition of substances such as sugar and salt decrease the water activity of the food to which they are added; that is why they act as food preservatives. Some species of yeast are **osmophilic**, i.e. they can grow in an environment supplying very little available moisture but which is high in sugar. Some bacteria can tolerate low a_w and high concentrations of salt. They are called **halophiles.**

Micro-organism	Minimum a_w for growth
Many bacteria	0.91
Many yeasts	0.88
Many moulds	0.80
Halophilic bacteria	0.75
Osmophilic yeasts	0.60

Table 12: Approximate minimum a_w for the growth of some micro-organisms

Temperature

Each micro-organism has:

◆ a maximum growth temperature
◆ an optimum growth temperature, i.e. the temperature at which it grows best and multiplies most rapidly
◆ a minimum growth temperature.

Microbes can be arbitrarily divided into three groups on the basis of their temperature requirements:

1   **Psychrophiles** (cold-loving organisms): can grow well at temperatures below 20°C, optimum growth range is 10°C to 20°C.

2   **Mesophiles** (organisms liking moderate temperatures): have an optimum growth temperature between 20°C and 45°C.

3   **Thermophiles** (organisms liking higher temperatures): can grow well at temperatures above 45°C; optimum growth range is 50°C to 60°C.

Some organisms may be able to resist the effect of high temperatures, even though they are not thermophilic; these are referred to as **thermoduric** (heat resisting) microbes. Similarly, organisms capable of surviving very low temperatures, although they are not psychrophilic, are called **psychrotrophic** (cold tolerant) microbes. An example of a psychrotrophic bacterium is *Listeria monocytogenes*.

Psychrophiles may cause spoilage of refrigerated foods, e.g. members of the bacterial genera *Achromobacter* and *Pseudomonas*. The majority of bacteria are mesophilic, especially the pathogenic bacteria, which have an optimum growth temperature of between 30°C–37°C. Moulds and yeasts are usually mesophilic or psychrophilic as they do not grow well at higher temperatures. Thermophilic bacteria are often troublesome in the dairy industry, since they may grow above pasteurisation temperatures.

Oxygen

The amount of oxygen available affects the growth of micro-organisms. Moulds are **aerobic** (i.e. require oxygen), while yeasts are either aerobic or **anaerobic**, depending on the conditions. Bacteria are classified into four groups, according to their oxygen requirements:

1   **Obligate aerobes**: can only grow if there is a plentiful supply of oxygen available.

2   **Obligate anaerobes**: can only grow if there is no oxygen present.

3   **Facultative anaerobes:** grow best if there is no oxygen present but they can also grow aerobically. These organisms are often simply termed **facultative**.

4   **Microaerophiles**: require the presence of oxygen, but they grow best when oxygen concentrations are less than normal.

Inorganic salts added to food can greatly affect the amount of oxygen available since they act as oxidising or reducing agents; e.g. potassium nitrate is used as a meat preservative, and increases the amount of oxygen available since it is an oxidising agent. The scale is logarithmic which means that there is a ten-fold difference between pH values; e.g. pH5 and pH6, pH6 and pH7.

pH

The **pH** of a substance is a measure of its acidity or alkalinity. It is measured on a scale of 0–14 with 0 being the most acidic and 14 being the most alkali. A pH of 7 is neutral, neither acid nor alkali.

Every micro-organism has a minimum, a maximum and an optimum pH for growth. Micro-organisms are significantly affected by the pH of food because they have no internal mechanism for controlling it. Most micro-organisms grow best if the pH of the food is between 6.6 and 7.5 (nearly neutral). They are said to be **neutrophilic** (neutral-loving). Bacteria, particularly pathogens, are less acid tolerant than moulds and yeasts, and there are no bacteria which

Micro-organism	Minimum pH
Moulds	0
Yeasts	1.5
Salmonella species	4.5
Staphylococcus aureus	4.0
Bacillus cereus	5.0
Colstridium botulinum	4.5
Clostridium perfringens	5.0
Listeria monocytogenes	4.4

Table 13: Approximate minimum pH for the growth of some micro-organisms

can grow if the pH is below 3.5. Therefore, the spoilage of high acid foods, such as fruit, is usually caused by yeasts and moulds.

Competition

When there are many different types of micro-organisms present on a food, they compete for nutrients. In conditions equally favourable for the growth of bacteria, moulds and yeasts, bacteria will grow faster than the yeasts which will grow faster than moulds. In addition, there will be competition between the different types of bacteria, yeasts and moulds. These interactions determine how food is spoiled. In fact, as food spoils, the growing micro-organisms cause the environment to change; e.g. *Lactobacillus* bacteria growing in milk produce lactic acid from the breakdown of lactose. The build up of this acid causes the pH to decrease, souring the milk. Eventually the pH becomes too low for the *Lactobacillus* to grow and other micro-organisms capable of growth at very low pHs take over and continue the spoilage process. This process is called **succession**.

SELF-CHECK QUESTIONS

1   *List the factors that affect the growth of micro-organisms.*
2   *Given ideal conditions, which grow faster from moulds, yeasts or bacteria?*

FOOD PRESERVATION

> By the end of this section you should be able to
> - list the main mechanisms of food preservation
> - describe how the main mechanisms of food preservation work

In order to prevent food spoilage, the growth of micro-organisms must be minimised or prevented. This can be achieved by removing one or more of the conditions necessary for growth or by providing conditions which interfere with microbial metabolism. Food preservation may be short-term or long-term and may be achieved in a variety of ways. Table 14 gives examples of the mechanisms used in some of the more common methods of food preservation. The various methods of food preservation are considered below.

Preservation method	Mechanisms controlling microbial growth
Freezing	Low temperatures Reduction in available moisture
Canning	High temperatures Sealed container Exculsion of oxygen
Modified atmosphere packing (MAP) of meats	Modification of gaseous atmosphere Low temperatures
Vacuum packaging	Reduction in available oxygen Sealed container Low temperatures

Table 14: Mechanisms by which some common food preservation methods control microbial growth

Heat treatment

By the end of this section you should be able to
- explain the differences between pasteurisation and sterilisation
- describe the various types of preservation methods used for milk

It is possible to destroy micro-organisms and their spores by holding food at a high temperature. The total destruction of micro-organisms (and their spores) by heat is known as **sterilisation**. The destruction of **pathogens** and most of the **spoilage organisms** present is called **pasteurisation**. This process uses lower temperatures than those used in the sterilisation of a food product, and is a short term means of food preservation. Cooking is a form of pasteurisation, since if the food is cooked properly the number of bacteria present will be reduced.

Sterilisation

This involves the use of heat to bring about the total destruction of all micro-organisms and their spores. Whilst heat is the most widely used method of achieving sterilisation of food, other techniques such as irradiation may be used. The most widespread use of heat as a sterilising agent is in the canning industry. The food is placed in a sealed container to prevent the entry of further spoilage organisms: a steel can coated with a thin layer of tin is the most common type of container. For some products (e.g. fruit), the can may be coated with lacquer as a further protection against corrosion. Glass bottles and jars are used as containers for some products, particularly jams and preserves. In recent years, flexible plastic containers have been used for a variety of liquid products, particularly milk and cream.

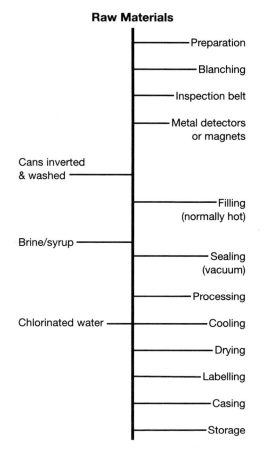

Figure 25: A schematic diagram of canning operations

The Canning Process

This involves the following operations:

1   **Cleaning and preparation**   All inedible parts are removed from the food and it is graded and washed.

2   **Blanching**   Most vegetable foods are blanched, either by being immersed in boiling water or by being exposed to steam. Blanching inactivates enzymes, which may affect the stability of the food while it awaits further processing. In addition, the blanching process helps to

drive out air bubbles trapped within the food, thus allowing a better 'fill'. If too much air remains in the cans, the desired temperature may not be reached during sterilisation and microbes may survive inside some of the cans.

3   **Filling and exhausting**   The washed, open cans are filled automatically with a weighed amount of the food. After filling, the cans are usually passed to an exhaust box in which they are exposed to hot water or steam. When the lid is sealed on, a partial vacuum will form in the can.

4   **Sealing**   Lids are placed on the cans and they are passed to an automatic sealing machine, which bends the edge of the lid and the flange on the can body into a roll. The roll is then flattened to form a hermetic (i.e. air tight) seal.

5   **Sterilisation**   The amount of heat required for adequate sterilisation depends on the following factors:

   a   size of can and nature of its contents (heat takes longer to penetrate into a large can); and

   b   type of food in the can and the pH of the food.

   The sterilisation process is designed to eliminate *Clostridium botulinum* and its spores, since this is the most dangerous heat-resistant microbe likely to be present in canned food. If this organism is destroyed then all other dangerous micro-organisms will also be killed. Normally for low acid foods, temperatures reached are 115°C–125°C.

6   **Cooling**   The can must be cooled slowly by gradually reducing the pressure of the steam used for heating. The cans are then cooled further using water. Since temporary leakage may occur at this point, it is imperative that the cooling water is clean and sterile.

Sterilisation of milk

According to the Dairy Products (Hygiene) Regulations 1995, milk may be sterilised in two ways:

1   **Continuous flow sterilisation process**   Milk is heat-treated to destroy all microbial cells and the majority of their spores. The milk will keep for at least a week without refrigeration. Milk is heated to between 105°C and 110°C for 20 to 40 minutes.

2   **The UHT (ultra heat treatment) process**   Here the milk is heated to a very high temperature for a very short time. Such a process kills all microbes and their spores without producing a marked effect on the flavour, colour and nutritive value of milk, as is the case of the continuous flow process. UHT milk is heated to 132°C and held there for one second. This milk is free from microbes and should keep unopened for at least six months.

Figure 26: A simplified diagram of the HTST pasteurisation process (see p. 112)

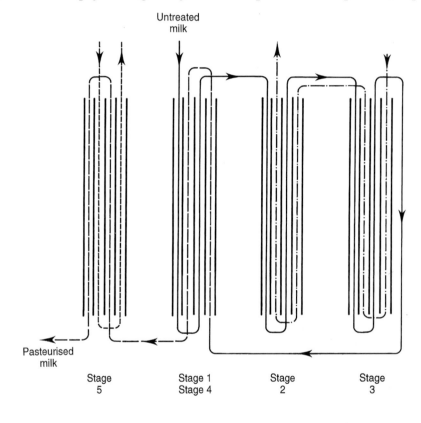

Key:

———— Incoming milk being pasteurised
— — — Outgoing milk being cooled
—·—·— Hot water
— — — — Cooling water

Stage 1 The incoming milk is being heated by milk which has already been pasteurised.

Stage 2 The temperature of the milk is raised to the temperature required for pasteurisation by means of hot water.

Stage 3 The milk is held at 72 °C for 15 seconds in order to achieve adequate pasteurisation.

Stage 4 The milk is partially cooled by giving up some of its heat to the cold incoming milk.

Stage 5 The milk is cooled to 10 °C or below by cooling water.

Pasteurisation

Pasteurisation extends the shelf-life of a food by using heat to reduce the number of spoilage organisms present. There are two processes permitted for the pasteurisation of milk:

1   **The holder process**   Milk is held at temperatures between 62.8°C and 65.6°C for 30 minutes and then rapidly cooled to below 10°C.

2   **The HTST (high temperature short time) process**   The milk is heated to a temperature of 71.7°C and held there for 15 seconds, and then cooled to below 10°C (see Figure 26, page 111). Both liquid egg and ice cream mix are pasteurised in order to eliminate possible pathogens, especially salmonellae.

SELF CHECK QUESTIONS

1   Why is pasteurisation only a short-term method of preserving food?
2   What are the stages involved in the production of canned foods?

THE USE OF LOW TEMPERATURES

By the end of this section you should be able to
- explain how freezing controls microbial growth
- explain why chilling is only a short term method of food preservation
- compare the benefits of cook chill and cook freeze systems

Foods may either be frozen at temperatures of less than 0°C or they may be held at chill temperatures (0°C–5°C) for much shorter periods of time. The actual length of time that frozen foods can be kept depends upon the temperature of storage.

Freezing

The preservation of foods by freezing involves two methods of controlling growth of micro-organisms.

1   The growth rate of microbes is reduced by the low temperature. At the same time, the rate of undesirable chemical changes is reduced considerably at low temperatures.

2   A large percentage of the water present in the food is converted to ice and is therefore unavailable to microbes (see the section on water activity, page 104)

Food should be frozen quickly. If food is frozen slowly, large ice crystals form which cause undesirable changes in the texture and appearance of the food. Quick freezing has been defined as that process in which the food passes through 0°C to −4°C in 30 minutes or less.

Most foods can be frozen successfully. In general, frozen food products are superior to canned foods since the product bears a closer resemblance to the fresh food. The nutritional value of the food is not seriously affected by the freezing process. In some cases the vitamin content of fresh frozen foods may be higher than that of fresh foods, since foods such as fruits and vegetables often lose vitamin C during transportation and storage.

Before freezing, all inedible parts of the food are usually removed. Fruits and vegetables are **blanched** in order to inactivate enzymes: blanching also reduces the number of bacteria present. Before freezing, substances may be added to the food; e.g. vitamin C, which reduces browning in fruit and vegetables, or antioxidants which prevent the oxidation of fat.

There are four main methods of freezing:

1   **Plate freezing**   The refrigerant passes through a number of hollow plates. The food is placed between the plates, e.g. fish fillets.

2   **Immersion freezing**   The food is placed directly into the refrigerant (which varies depending upon the type of food being frozen). Brine is sometimes used, especially for fish, whereas sugar solutions are often used for fruit and vegetables. In more modern processes, liquid nitrogen can be used (e.g. for raspberries and prawns).

3   **Blast freezing**   A blast of very cold air is blown directly onto the food.

4   **Fluidised bed freezing**   This method is very successful for freezing foods which are of small particle size, such as peas. It is an adaptation of blast freezing in which the air is blown upwards through mesh over which the food is passing. The air speed is controlled so that the solid particles of food flow as if they were liquid.

Chilling

The food is placed at a temperature above the freezing point of water. The temperature inside a refrigerator or chiller should be in the range of 0–4°C. At these temperatures the growth of micro-organisms is slowed although there is increasing concern about a number of bacterial pathogens, e.g. *Listeria monocytogenes*, *Yersinia enterocolitica*, and *Aeromonas hydrophilia* which can grow, albeit slowly, at refrigeration temperatures. Many moulds including *Penicillium*, are capable of growth at refrigeration temperatures and may be responsible for the spoilage of chilled foods.

Cook chill catering systems

Cook chill systems involve the rapid chilling of pre-cooked foods to less than 3°C in less than 90 minutes. The products are held refrigerated until required. Products are then regenerated (i.e. reheated) just prior to serving. The advantages of the system include efficient purchasing, increased productivity and the elimination of unsociable working hours. Food items can be stored for up to five days, including the days of production and use, given that appropriate temperature control is maintained. For more details of the cook chill catering system, see the Department of Health's publication listed in the Useful Publications list (page 198).

'Sous-vide' or 'cuisine en papillote sous-vide' is a modified version of the cook chill system. 'Sous-vide' uses high quality raw or par-cooked ingredients which are packaged into plastic pouches, sealed under vacuum and heat treated (pasteurised). The pasteurised product is rapidly chilled and stored until required. Products are reheated after a period of chilled storage. The advantages of this system are the extended shelf-life and quality of the products.

Cook freeze systems, like cook chill systems, involve the bulk production of foods for storage and subsequent regeneration. In this case the foods are frozen and thus have a longer shelf-life than cook chill products. The advantages of the system are similar to those for the cook chill system. Cook freeze systems are less widely used due to problems with the quality of the final product caused by uneven freezing, as well as the added difficulties of thawing the product before use.

SELF CHECK QUESTIONS

1   *What is cuisine en papillote sous-vide?*
2   *Describe the four main methods of freezing food.*

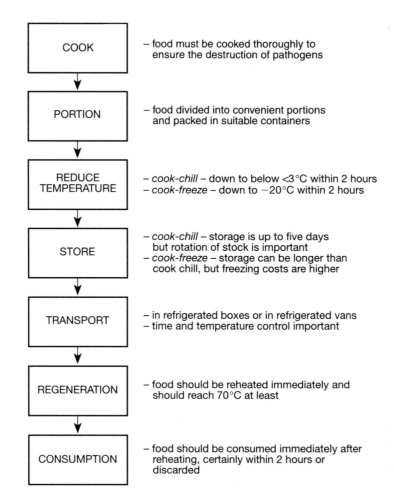

COOK	– food must be cooked thoroughly to ensure the destruction of pathogens
PORTION	– food divided into convenient portions and packed in suitable containers
REDUCE TEMPERATURE	– *cook-chill* – down to below <3°C within 2 hours – *cook-freeze* – down to −20°C within 2 hours
STORE	– *cook-chill* – storage is up to five days but rotation of stock is important – *cook-freeze* – storage can be longer than cook chill, but freezing costs are higher
TRANSPORT	– in refrigerated boxes or in refrigerated vans – time and temperature control important
REGENERATION	– food should be reheated immediately and should reach 70°C at least
CONSUMPTION	– food should be consumed immediately after reheating, certainly within 2 hours or discarded

Figure 27: The cook-chill and cook-freeze catering systems

THE REMOVAL OF MOISTURE (DRYING)

By the end of this section you should be able to
● describe the various mechanisms by which food can be dried

In order to prevent the growth of micro-organisms in a food, the water activity of the food must be reduced to 0.6 or below. Don't forget that bacterial spores may survive in dried products and germinate on reconstitution of the product, e.g. *Bacillus cereus* in rice. Sun-drying is one of the oldest preservation methods known to man and is widely used in hot climates. The modern process of dehydration consists of the removal of moisture from the food by the application of heat, usually in the presence of a controlled flow of air. It is important that the temperature used is not too high, since this will cause undesirable changes in the food, and hardening. Sometimes additional means to control growth are used, e.g. smoking and salting.

Before drying, food undergoes a variety of treatments. In the case of vegetables this includes washing, grading and blanching (to destroy enzymes). Sodium sulphite is usually added to the blanching water, which improves the colour of the product, aids vitamin C retention and destroys some of the microbes. Other foods such as meats may be cooked prior to dehydration.

1   **Tunnel drying**   In this method the food is placed on conveyor belts or perforated trays and passed through a warm air tunnel. A more modern development is fluidised bed drying in which warm air is blown upwards and the particles of food are kept in motion. This method is particularly used for vegetables.

2   **Spray drying**   This method is used for drying fairly liquid foods such as milk and eggs. The food enters the top of a large drying chamber as a fine spray. The spray mixes with warm air, the water evaporates and a fine powder is produced which is removed from the bottom of the chamber.

3   **Roller drying**   The food is applied in paste form as a thin film to the surface of a revolving heated roller or drum. As the drum rotates, the food dries and the dried product is removed from the drum by a scraper knife. Products dried by this method include instant breakfast cereals and potatoes.

4   **Freeze drying**   The food is first frozen and then subjected to a mild heat treatment under vacuum. Under reduced pressure, the ice crystals which form during the freezing stage change directly from ice to water vapour, without passing through the liquid phase. This results in a product which is porous and very little changed in size and shape from the original food. Since little heat damage occurs, the colour, flavour and nutrient content of freeze dried products are affected less than in some other methods of drying. As freeze dried products are porous they can be rapidly reconstituted in cold water. A wide variety of foods can be dried by this method, e.g. meat, shellfish, fruits and vegetables.

SELF CHECK QUESTION

I   *Describe the main methods used to dry foods.*

THE USE OF CHEMICAL PRESERVATIVES

By the end of this section you should be able to
- list some examples of chemicals used to preserve foods

The main chemicals used to preserve food include:

1   **Curing**   The curing of meats such as bacon involves using a brine solution composed of sodium chloride (25%), potassium nitrate (1%) and sodium nitrite (0.1%). The meat may be soaked in the brine, or the brine may be injected into the meat by hollow needles. The salt content inhibits microbial growth and the meat develops a characteristic colour and flavour. Some cured products (e.g. herring and bacon) are also smoked by exposing them to smoke from a wood fire. The smoke contains antimicrobial substances which reduce spoilage. It also gives the food a characteristic taste.

2   **Preserving with sugar**   Many fruit products, such as jams and crystallised fruits, are preserved with sugar. Sugar reduces microbial activity due to its dehydrating effect.

3   **Addition of acid**   There are two methods of adding acid. The food may be pickled, i.e. soaked in an acid solution such as vinegar (acetic acid), or the food may be inoculated with a culture of selected bacteria which produce acidic products. Foods such as yoghurt and sauerkraut (fermented cabbage) are produced in this way.

4   **Other chemical preservatives**   There are 35 preservatives which are permitted in the UK. All of these except one (nisin) are also permitted in the EU. The use of chemicals to preserve food is controlled by the Preservatives in Food Regulations 1979. Some examples of permitted preservatives and their uses in food is given in Table 15, page 118.

SELF CHECK QUESTIONS

1   *How do sugar and salt preserve foods?*
2   *Name two other chemicals used to preserve food. Give examples of the types of food they may be used in.*

Preservative	Example of Use
E200 sorbic acid	Soft drinks, fruit yoghurt, processed cheese slices
E201 sodium sorbate E202 potassium sorbate	Frozen pizza, flour confectionery
E220 sulphur dioxide E221 sodium sulphate	Dried fruit, dehydrated vegetables, fruit juices and syrups, sausages, cider, beer and wine
E249 potassium nitrite E250 sodium nitrite E280 propionic acid E281 sodium propionate	Bacon, ham, cured meats, meat, pastes, corned beef Bread and flour confectionery Christmas pudding

For further information about permitted preservatives see the Food Sense booklet, *About Food Additives*.

Table 15: Some permitted preservatives and examples of their use

PRESERVING FOOD USING IONISING RADIATION

By the end of this section you should be able to
- describe how foods are preserved using ionising radiation
- give examples of the types of food which may be preserved in this way

The initial research on the preservation of food by the use of radiation demonstrated that it was impossible to eliminate all microbes without causing undesirable changes in the food itself. Bacterial spores are often very resistant and were found to survive large doses of radiation. However, further research has led to the development of a variety of processes which can be used in food preservation.

The two main types of ionising radiation use are:

◆ gamma (γ) rays from radioactive cobalt 60 or caesium 137
◆ beams of electrons from radioactive substances produced by linear accelerators.

Purpose	Dose (kGy)	Products
Low dose (up to 2kGy)		
Inhibition of sprouting	0.05–0.15	Potatoes, onions, garlic, ginger
Killing insects and parasites	0.15–0.50	Cereals and pulses, fresh and dried fruits, dried fish and meat
Control or delay of ripening	0.50–1.0	Fresh fruit and vegetables
Medium dose (1–10kGy)		
Extension of food shelf life	1.5–3.0	Fresh fish, strawberries
Destruction of spoilage and pathogenic micro-organism	2.0–5.0	Fresh and frozen seafood, poultry and meat in raw or frozen state
Improving physical properties of food	2.0–7.0	Grapes (increasing juice yield), dehydrated vegetables (reducing cooking time)
High dose (10–50kGy)		
Commercial sterilisation (in combination with mild heat)	30–50	Meat, poultry, seafood, prepared foods, sterilised hospital diets
Decontamination of certain food additives and ingredients	10–50	Spices, enzyme preparations

Table 16: Food irradiation treatments

Gamma rays are highly penetrating and are capable of passing through large containers of foods. Thus, food can be treated in its final packaging or even in pallet loads. Electron beams have less penetrating power than gamma rays and are suitable only for foods less than 5cm thick. Such treatment is ideal for food which can be transported in a thin layer and at high speed, such as grain and spices.

The treatment of food by ionising radiation does not produce any significant change in the temperature of the food. Irradiation therefore can be used as a 'cold' preservation process, killing insects and heat sensitive micro-organisms in foods such as spices, enzyme preparations and frozen foods.

SELF CHECK QUESTIONS

1 *How are ionising radiations measured?*
2 *What types of food are most suitable for preservation in this way?*

SHORT-TERM PRESERVATION METHODS

By the end of this section you should be able to
● list different methods of short term preservation

1 **Conventional methods of cooking using heat**   Adequate heat treatment will reduce the number of microbes and kill pathogens; e.g. grilling, roasting, stewing, braising.

2 **Use of microwaves**   Microwave ovens preserve food in two ways:

   a   internal generation of heat reduces the numbers of microbes present

   b   microwaves themselves have a lethal effect on microbes.

3 **Chilling**   The temperatures used for chilling vary considerably. They depend on the nature of the product and the storage atmosphere; e.g. bananas are stored best at 15°C, whereas meat is stored at 1°C to 2°C.

4 **Controlled atmosphere storage**   This involves controlling the humidity and composition of the atmosphere, and is normally used in conjunction with chilling. The optimum humidity depends on the food stored and the temperature of storage. Excessive humidity encourages microbial growth, while too low a humidity results in loss of moisture and in vegetables wilting. The composition of the atmosphere affects storage. If the level of carbon dioxide in the air is increased, the rate of spoilage is reduced. The optimum concentration of carbon dioxide depends on the type of food stored. Concentrations of 10% CO_2 are used for meat, while between 5% and 10% is best for vegetables and 2.5% for eggs.

5 **Exclusion of oxygen**   Methods such as vacuum packing prevent the growth of moulds and aerobic bacteria, but yeasts can respire anaerobically and many pathogenic bacteria are anaerobic or facultative. Therefore, this may only be used as a means of preservation if other methods are also used, e.g. destruction by heat.

SELF-CHECK QUESTIONS

I   *List the ways in which temperature can be used to preserve foods.*
2   *How do microwaves preserve food?*

FOOD SPOILAGE

By the end of this section you should be able to
- define spoiled food
- describe how a range of foods spoil

In most cases, micro-organisms use our food as a source of nutrients for their own growth. This can result in the deterioration of the product resulting in what we recognise as **spoiled food**. In order to grow, micro-organisms must convert the complex forms of carbon, nitrogen and sulphur found in dead plant and animal material into simpler forms which they can use, and as a result food is spoiled. Clearly, food spoilage is a natural process. Food producers and manufacturers aim to prevent or reduce the actions of micro-organisms and increase the shelf-life of our food by:

◆ minimising the contact between our food and micro-organisms
◆ eliminating micro-organisms from our food
◆ manipulating conditions to prevent or reduce microbial growth (preservation).

When food spoilage takes place, two distinct processes are involved:

1   **Autolysis**   This word means self-destruction and is used to describe the cellular breakdown caused by enzymes contained within the food itself. This breakdown starts immediately after slaughter or harvest. In many instances, a limited amount of enzyme activity may be beneficial, e.g. in the ripening of fruit and the tenderisation of meat. However, in most instances autolysis is detrimental.

2   **Microbial Spoilage**   Once food is bruised or damaged in some way, the food is vulnerable to attack by microbes. The main agents of microbial spoilage are bacteria, moulds and yeasts. These organisms break down the complex organic components of the food into simpler compounds and so cause alterations in the flavour, texture, colour and smell of the food.

The basic principles of food spoilage

Spoiled food may be defined as *food that has been damaged or injured such that it is unfit for human consumption.* However, the point at which food becomes spoiled will depend upon the opinion of the person judging it. For example, some British people like to eat their game meats such as pheasant and hare 'high', having allowed that characteristic strong flavour to develop by hanging or ageing the meat. Most Americans would call this meat spoiled. The buried fish, titmuck, considered a delicacy and eaten by Eskimos, is a smelly, semi-liquid product which most of us would consider inedible.

Despite these differences, there are a set of criteria which most individuals would agree characterises 'fit food':

1   The desired stage of development or maturity: e.g. fruits should be at a certain stage of ripeness, poultry should be from young birds.

2   Freedom from pollution at any stage in production or handling: e.g. vegetables should not be consumed raw if they have been fertilised with raw sewage; molluscan shellfish should be rejected if they have been grown in sewage contaminated waters. Freedom from objectionable change in a food often resulting from microbial attack.

However, not all microbial change is objectionable. Mould growth in many cheeses is desirable, but on fruit it may be undesirable. Some changes may be deemed undesirable, such as limp lettuce or soft flabby carrots, when in fact little or no microbial damage has taken place, but the changes in appearance and texture are sufficient to put us off the food.

EXERCISE

Gather a range of foodstuffs which are showing signs of spoilage. Record the name of the food and the initial signs of spoilage on a chart together with the date. Put the food into appropriate containers* and allow it to spoil over time. Record the changes over as long a period as is practical (see safety note below). You could use a range of different foodstuffs to illustrate the different types of spoilage which occur. You could also vary the temperatures at which you store the food to see what effect this has on the rate and types of spoilage which occur. The following foods will give some interesting comparisons:

- ◆ Milk – compare the spoilage of fresh pasteurised and raw milk
- ◆ Meat – compare the spoilage of minced beef and steak
- ◆ Fruit – oranges, pears, apples or soft fruits
- ◆ Vegetables – root vegetables e.g. carrots, salad items e.g. cucumber

Try to obtain canned foods that have spoiled. What are the signs to look for here?

* Remember: the type of container may itself affect spoilage by influencing one or more of the factors that affect microbial growth. Can you use this to your advantage?

*Safety note: **DO NOT DO THIS IN A KITCHEN** – Remember that by spoiling food you are encouraging micro-organisms to grow. Remember too that spoiled food can smell quite strongly, so there will be a limit to how long you can keep products without complaint.*

The spoilage of fruit and vegetables

Unlike many other foodstuffs, fruits and vegetables are 'alive' for a period of time after harvesting and before processing. This enables them to be picked unripe and extends the shelf-life of the product. Most spoilage occurs as a result of damage during transportation and storage. Because of its low pH, fruit is most commonly spoiled by moulds and yeasts. Vegetables tend to be spoiled by moulds or bacteria.

The spoilage of raw meats and fish

Raw meat changes due to autolysis during the ageing process prior to sale. Subsequent changes are usually bacterial, with the exact type of spoilage depending upon the type of meat. Bacterial growth may sometimes be visible as a fluorescent sheen on the surface of some meats, particularly pork.

Fish is also spoiled by a combination of autolysis and bacterial activity. It is considered more perishable than meats because of the rapid rate at which autolytic changes occur, hence it is always chilled or kept packed in ice.

The spoilage of milk

Milk is an excellent growth medium for many different types of micro-organisms. Generally milk is considered spoiled when it sours, especially if it has curdled. These changes are caused by the growth of bacteria which are present in the raw milk and which survive pasteurisation. If allowed to continue spoiling, further changes result in the growth of moulds on the surface of the curdled product.

The spoilage of bakery products

Bread and other bakery products are most likely to be spoiled by mould and sometimes yeasts. This is due to the low levels of moisture and sometimes to the high levels of sugar in these products. Bacteria can cause 'rope' in bread: this is more common in home baked bread. The ropiness is caused by the bacteria *Bacillus subtilis*. It produces strands of a sticky slime which have a characteristically sweet odour. The ropey area is orange to brown in colour and if it is cut into the slimy material can be drawn into long strands (the rope).

The spoilage of canned products

The main reasons for spoilage of canned foods are:

◆ insufficient sterilisation which means that spores of anaerobic bacteria may survive and germinate

◆ leakage which is due either to a badly made can or a can which has been improperly sealed

◆ erosion of the can which is often caused by the acidity of the contents.

The most common types of spoilage are:

1   **Thermophilic gas spoilage**   This is usually caused by anaerobic spore forming bacteria such as the genus *Clostridium*. This type of spoilage occurs in cans of low acid foods which have been insufficiently sterilised. Usually large amounts of hydrogen are produced, and this gas causes the cans to swell.

2   **Carbon dioxide gas spoilage**   Non-spore-forming bacteria may enter the can after sterilisation. In this case the contents of the can often appear slimy and frothy.

3   **Flat sour spoilage**   Some species of bacteria which produce heat-resistant spores (e.g. *Bacillus*) may survive if the heat treatment is not sufficient. They do not produce any marked damage in the appearance of the food but they ferment the food, producing acid, which gives the food a disagreeable taste.

SELF-CHECK QUESTIONS

1   *How can you tell if a food item is spoiled?*
2   *List the ways in which bread can spoil.*
3   *Describe how meat usually spoils.*

Food Hygiene and the food we eat

This chapter examines the food storage mechanisms by which the shelf life of foods can be extended. It also examines the various types of food contamination which may reduce the keeping quality of food and render it unfit for human consumption. The final section of the chapter examines the range of micro-organisms which cause food poisoning, potentially the most serious food contaminants.

PRINCIPLES OF THE SAFE STORAGE OF FOOD

By the end of this section you should be able to
- describe the range of food storage facilities necessary in a catering operation
- safely store food in a refrigerator
- explain the star marking system for freezer cabinets

EXERCISE

Find out when the main food deliveries take place at your college or place of work and get permission to observe them. Record accurately the delivery procedures for all types of food. In your opinion, are the procedures you have observed adequate? Outline how you would modify procedures to make them more effective.

Most catering operations bulk-purchase foods, many of which come pre- or part prepared. For example, cook-chill operations often purchase pre-diced meats and pre-peeled and sliced vegetables to cut down on both preparation times and the 'dirty' operations within the unit. Whilst the majority of these items are purchased on a daily or as required basis to maximise the freshness and quality of the products, it is important that the foods are stored correctly until required.

The correct storage of foods in a catering operation is essential to the economics of food production and particularly to hygiene. A failure to store food correctly will ultimately lead to spoiled food and to a significant reduction in the shelf-life of any food item. It may also encourage pest infestations. It is therefore critical that food is stored at the correct temperature and humidity and that the integrity of packaging and visual condition of the food is monitored prior to storage.

Remember that all our food begins to decompose gradually on harvesting or after slaughter. The aim of food storage is to reduce the rate at which food decomposes. Thus it is important that during storage it is not exposed to further contamination or to conditions which might exacerbate the decomposition of that product.

All food operations should have the facilities to store dry goods, fruit and vegetables, refrigerated and frozen foods.

Dry food stores

A dry food store should be cool, dry, well ventilated, well lit and vermin proof. The internal finish should be smooth and impervious so that it is easy to clean. Any shelving should be raised from the floor to facilitate this process. All shelving should also be readily cleanable. Cupboards should be avoided as they provide potential havens for pests.

The types of food items likely to be found in a dry food store include dried foods (pastas, rice, pastry mixes etc.), flours and cereals, canned goods and other non-perishable items. Flours and cereals should be stored in lidded bins rather that in the original sacks. The bins should be checked for signs of pest infestation on a regular basis. They should be cleaned regularly, and not topped up.

A First In First Out (FIFO) system should be adopted for all goods to ensure that stock rotation is maintained. Shallow shelving may facilitate this as it will minimise the likelihood of products becoming lost at the back of the shelf. The integrity of packaging on all food items should be checked prior to storage and the routine inspection of any canned or boxed products on a regular basis will give early warnings of possible pest infestations. Canned products should also be checked for signs of rust, which may indicate that the humidity of the store is too high.

Fruit and vegetable stores

Very few fruits and vegetables need refrigerated storage. While most catering operations purchase these commodities on a daily basis, it is likely that smaller operations will store root vegetables and possibly some fruits. As with a dry food store, a clean well-ventilated storage area is necessary, fitted with stainless steel shelving. It is usually appropriate to store fruit and vegetables in the containers (usually boxes) in which they are delivered, as this reduces handling (which may increase the rate of spoilage). However, it is particularly important that these products are thoroughly and carefully inspected on receipt, as 'one bad apple in a box' will rapidly spoil the rest. There have also been incidents of unusual infestations from exotic insects including tarantulas, and of greater concern, cockroaches in boxes of fruit.

Refrigerated stores

EXERCISE

As you have seen in the previous chapter, the temperature at which food is kept affects the rate and type of food spoilage which occurs. Temperature control is the most widely used means of slowing food spoilage. Before you read this section, record the temperatures of all the food storage areas in the kitchen. The refrigerators and freezers may well be linked to an automatic temperature recorder which can provide you with a print out of the temperatures for the previous 24 hours. But don't forget to record temperatures of all the other storage areas too. What other factors will affect the rate of food spoilage? Can you record these too?

Refrigerators are used for the short-term storage of high-risk perishable foods such as fresh meats and dairy products. Temperatures of less than 5°C slow the growth of, or prevent toxin formation by, most of the common food poisoning bacteria. There is however increasing concern about certain psychotrophic pathogens which are able to grow at refrigeration temperatures. These organisms include *Listeria monocytogenes, Yersinia enterocolitica, Clostridium botulinum* type E, and *Aeromonas hydrophilia*. Growth of these organisms is slow at very low temperatures, so short term storage should not cause problems given low levels of contamination, but the temperature of the refrigerator should be as low as possible.

Temperature control is the most important factor in controlling the growth of bacteria, and to ensure efficient temperature control in the refrigerator it is important to ensure that it is sited correctly and is operating properly. Refrigerators should be sited in a readily accessible point in the kitchen as far away from any heat source (e.g. range) as is practical. They should also be out of any direct sunlight again to minimise the 'work' the refrigerator has to do when it is hot. The motor should be well ventilated and accessible for cleaning. The construction of the refrigerator should facilitate cleaning and the door seals should be checked regularly to ensure both cleanliness and their integrity. Walk-in chill stores should be fitted with air curtains or plastic strip doors and should have self-closing doors to help maintain the internal temperature. There should be sufficient refrigerator capacity to cope adequately with peak demand although this means that there will usually be additional space. This also means that stored items can be adequately spaced to allow for maximal air flow around products which helps maintain the temperature of the stored foods.

All refrigerators should be set to operate at between 0–4°C. At these temperatures the growth of food poisoning bacteria and spoilage organisms is minimised. As you learned in Chapter 7, the greater the temperature, the more quickly organisms grow. Additionally, if the temperature of the refrigerator is higher then it takes longer to cool food placed into it adequately: it prolongs the time the food is in the **danger zone**. The danger zone is the temperature range within which bacteria will most readily multiply, i.e. between 5°C–63°C. A thermometer should be positioned in the warmest part of the refrigerator and readings should be taken and recorded at least once a day. If the refrigerator is fitted with a remote temperature sensor, the record of daily temperature fluctuations should be seen by those who supervise use of the equipment. This means that any irregularities will be noticed and minor problems can be dealt with before they become major ones.

The coldest part of the refrigerator varies according to whether it is a fridge/freezer, an ice box fridge or a frost free fridge.

1   **Fridge/freezers** are likely to be coldest in the area above the salad bin, usually the lower two shelves.

2   **Ice box fridges** are usually coldest on the top and middle shelves.

3   **Frost free fridges** should be equally cold throughout as air is circulated throughout the cabinet. In this respect these fridges are much more like the commercial designs which maintain an even distribution of cold air throughout the cabinet.

Check the manufacturer's guide to your equipment, as this should tell you where the coldest part of your fridge is.

To maintain the temperature of the refrigerator, it is important to maintain the

cleanliness of the door seal and to keep the door closed as far as possible.
Never place hot food into a refrigerator because it will:

◆ raise the internal temperature
◆ raise the temperature of food already in the refrigerator
◆ increase the rate of bacterial growth
◆ increase condensation and the potential for drip (**cross-contamination**)
◆ increase ice build-up on the cooling unit.

It is critical that cross-contamination is not facilitated by the storage of food in
a refrigerator. Ideally there should be separate refrigerators for raw, cooked and

1 Fruit, vegetables, salad items should be stored in the salad drawer.

2 Milk, fruit juices should be stored in the bottle rack in the door. This will, however, depend on the design of your 'fridge.

3 Butter, lard, margarines, cheese, preserves, salad dressings, spreads, sauces, eggs, should be stored on the centre
   or top shelves.

4 Fresh meat, cooked meat, ham, sausages, milk products, cream, fish, should be stored above the salad drawer. NB.
   package meats separately. Store raw meat and poultry below cooked meats and dairy products.

5 Convenience foods and cooked items should be stored on top or centre shelves.

Figure 28: The storage of food in a refrigerator

dairy foods, but if this is not practical, additional care must be taken when putting food into the refrigerator. The following rules should be observed:

1   All foods should be placed into clean labelled, lidded containers for storage.

2   Open tins of food should not be placed into the refrigerator. Many canned foods contain acids which will damage the can and cause contamination and spoilage (taint). The best example of this is canned tomatoes.

3   **High-risk** and cooked foods should be placed on shelves above raw foods.

4   A shelf which has been previously used for the storage of raw foods should not be used for the storage of cooked foods without disinfection. It is advisable to label the shelf according to its intended use.

5   An efficient and effective system of stock rotation must be implemented to avoid foods being stored past their use by dates

The storage of frozen food

Most domestic and commercial catering freezers operate at temperatures of about −18°C. At this temperature food will not keep indefinitely. The shelf-life will depend upon the initial number of micro-organisms present, the times and temperatures of any distribution and the final storage temperature.

All frozen foods must be checked upon receipt for signs of thawing as this indicates poor temperature control during distribution. Products should be temperature checked and should be rejected if the temperature is less than −12°C. Thawed or thawing products should not be accepted. Similarly, the issue of frozen foods from a freezer store to the kitchen should be controlled so that products intended to remain frozen do so until they are used.

Some freezer compartments may be marked with the star system which indicates the temperature and times of storage in the labelled compartment (Figure 29).

Freezers should, where possible be fitted with an alarm system that signals a power failure or breakdown. They should also be fitted with an automatic temperature monitoring device that records the temperature profile of the cabinet during a 24 hour period. Should frozen food become partially or

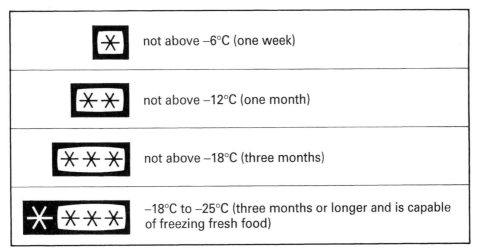

Figure 29: The star marking system for freezer compartments

completely thawed, then the food may in certain circumstances be treated as fresh and used immediately. If there is any doubt as to the length of time the food has been thawed, then it should be discarded. Sometimes it may be possible to cook thawed raw products and to refreeze the cooked item.

In the event of freezer breakdown the freezer should not be opened. Cover it with thick blankets and/or newspapers to further insulate it and leave it until repaired.

FOOD CONTAMINATION

> By the end of this section you should be able to
> - list the major groups of food contaminants and give examples
> - describe the main causes of physical, chemical and biological food contamination
> - explain how bacteria contaminate food
> - define the terms high risk food, vehicle and cross contamination

In addition to maximising the shelf-life of foods, appropriate storage helps to minimise the risks of food contamination. Food contamination may be defined as the presence of any unacceptable matter in food. This may be the presence of bacteria or other micro-organisms, metal, glass, poisons or anything else which makes the food unacceptable. There are three types of contamination:

◆ physical
◆ chemical
◆ biological.

Physical contamination

Food may be contaminated by **foreign bodies** at any stage during its production and preparation. A common source of foreign body contamination are workers who allow nails, nuts and bolts, paint flakes etc. to fall into food. Other types of physical contamination may be glass, string, polythene, cigarette ends, and items which fall from food handlers' pockets e.g. pens, combs or money, or from their person e.g. earrings, hair ornaments or even plasters.

In the larger food operations, metal detectors are often used to pick up any metallic items in food. These do not of course identify contamination by non-metallic items, and extreme vigilance is needed by food handlers to prevent this type of food contamination.

Chemical contamination

Chemical contamination is where unwanted and sometimes dangerous chemicals contaminate food. It can happen at any point during food production from growth; e.g. pesticides used at a point too close to harvest, so that residues remain in the grain through to preparation; or contamination with cleaning chemicals. Chemical contamination can't generally be seen although it may cause food to smell strange. It can cause acute illness or long term and often more serious illness. It is therefore important that food is protected from chemical contamination and the following basic rules should be followed:

◆ always store chemicals in the containers they are supplied in
◆ store chemical away from foods, preferably in a lockable cupboard or room
◆ dispose of chemicals safely.

Biological contamination

Biological contamination can be divided into microbiological and non-microbiological contamination:

1 **Microbiological contamination** consists of contamination of food by unwanted micro-organisms, usually moulds, bacteria and viruses. This type of contamination often occurs in food premises because of the ignorance or laziness of food handlers, or due to inadequate space or poor premises design.

2 **Non-microbiological contamination** includes contamination by insects, rodents, animals and birds. All of these may contaminate food by

defecating in it, eating it, losing fur or feathers in it or dying in it. Such contamination may also be classified as physical contamination because it can be seen and could be 'picked out' of the food.

Mould spores are always present in the atmosphere and on surfaces. To prevent mould contamination, foods should always be covered and mouldy foods thrown away. As moulds will grow rapidly in humid or damp environments, good ventilation is important in a kitchen. Yeasts are also present in the air and can be a significant problem for bakeries and breweries. They are a less significant problem in other areas.

Viruses are generally brought into a food preparation environment by food handlers who are **carriers,** or on raw foods (e.g. shellfish).

Bacterial contamination is the most important type of microbiological contamination. It may occur as a result of poor personal hygiene, poor food handling practices, pests or environmental contamination from dust or soil.

Routes of bacterial contamination

Bacteria are unable to move from place to place unaided. Whilst they are sometimes transferred from the source directly into the **high-risk** food, more often they are moved indirectly by one or more **vehicles.** A **vehicle** is anything which can transfer bacteria from its source to a high risk food. Some common examples are knives used firstly to cut raw meat and then to cut cooked meat without being washed in-between. This type of transfer is called **cross-contamination**. The cutting board used for these meats may also be a vehicle of cross-contamination. The cloth used to wipe over the board before it is finally put away also becomes a vehicle as do the food handler's hands. Your hands are perhaps the most dangerous vehicle as they not only pick-up bacteria from food but may also contaminate foods with bacteria from other sources; e.g. bacteria transferred to the hands after using the toilet will be passed onto food if you do not wash your hands thoroughly. As a result of bacterial contamination of foods, illness may occur in the consumer. This is called food poisoning.

FOOD POISONING

By the end of this section you should be able to
- give examples of chemical causes of food poisoning
- describe the different ways in which bacteria can cause food poisoning
- describe the main sources, symptoms and control measures for the common causes of bacterial food poisonings

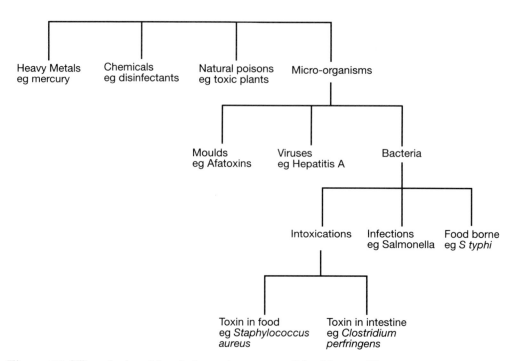

Figure 30: The relationship of the major causes of food borne illness

Food poisoning may be caused by the consumption of foods contaminated with moulds, viruses, bacteria or their toxins or chemicals. It may also occur as the result of eating naturally toxic plants and animals (Figure 30).

Chemical food poisoning

Chemical contamination of food may be accidental or unforeseen, e.g. the contamination of harvested grain with pesticide residues, and the contamination of fish by waste chemicals in polluted water. Chemical contamination of our food may also be deliberate: e.g. the use of chemical additives and preservatives. These compounds undergo rigorous testing before they can be added to our food, and generally do not cause problems. Occasionally however, the consumption of large amounts can cause illness; e.g. monosodium glutamate (MSG) can cause illness if consumed in very large amounts.

The consumption of food crops contaminated with heavy metals may also lead to illness. Copper, lead, tin, zinc, aluminium and mercury can all cause illness if ingested in sufficient amounts. The effects of these metals is often cumulative and it may be difficult to pinpoint the exact cause of illness.

Food poisoning caused by toxic plants and animals

Food poisoning caused by the consumption of poisonous plants is very rare in catering operations. It usually occurs as a result of individuals mistaking a poisonous plant for a non-poisonous plant. Children are at risk as they may eat for example the berries of deadly nightshade, mistaking them for blackberries. Other common and often fatal errors occur as a result of mistaking edible fungi for more toxic varieties.

Some plant foods are toxic when raw but quite safe when cooked. A good example of these are red kidney beans which contain a **haemagglutinin** that must be boiled for ten minutes to inactivate it. Consumption of inadequately cooked kidney beans may cause nausea, vomiting and diarrhoea within one to six hours after consumption of the beans.

A variety of animal foods (especially fish) contain toxic parts which must be removed before eating. The dead men's fingers (the nervous tissue) of crabs and the intestines of puffer fish (a Japanese delicacy) are highly toxic and must be carefully removed before the fish is eaten. Other fish can cause illness if they are consumed at the wrong time of year or after inappropriate storage.

Scombrotoxic poisoning

Among the scombroid fish are tuna, mackerel, bonito and many others. Illness occurs when fish containing high levels of histamine (scombrotoxin) are eaten. The histamine is produced in the fish by bacterial activity. Sufficient levels of histamine may be produced without unacceptable changes in the sensory quality of the fish, although more often they are accompanied by changes in odour. Histamine production occurs more rapidly when the fish is stored above refrigerator temperatures. The lowest temperature for the production of histamine appears to be around 7°C, although this depends upon the types of bacteria involved.

Symptoms of scombroid poisoning occur within minutes and for up to three hours after the ingestion of the fish; most cases occur within one hour. Symptoms include flushing of the face and neck, accompanied by a feeling of intense heat, general non-specific discomfort and diarrhoea. Facial and neck rashes subsequently develop as do intense, throbbing headaches which fade to a continuous dull ache. Other symptoms include dizziness, fainting, burning of the mouth and throat and an inability to swallow.

Paralytic shellfish poisoning

This condition is contracted by eating toxic oysters, mussels or clams. These shellfish become toxic after feeding on certain plankton. Symptoms usually develop within 30 minutes of eating contaminated shellfish. Symptoms are characterised by a tingling numbness or burning sensation which begins in the mouth, lips and tongue and spreads across the face, neck and scalp and then to the fingers and toes. A fatal dose of the poison may be obtained from eating a single serving of highly toxic shellfish. In humans it has a mortality rate of 1–22%.

Prevention of this type of poisoning consists of avoiding seafood from waters laden with the toxic plankton. In addition, the hazard can be reduced by heating above 100°C. Thorough cooking may reduce the toxin by as much as 70%.

Food poisoning caused by moulds and viruses

Moulds

A large number of moulds have been demonstrated to produce toxins called **mycotoxins**. Some are potentially carcinogenic, some display specificity for certain organs and some are toxic by other mechanisms, not all of which are fully understood. In the early 1980s, 14 mycotoxins were found to be potential human carcinogens, the most potent being the **aflatoxins**.

The existence of aflatoxins was discovered in the 1960s when more than 100,000 turkeys died in England after eating peanut meal imported from Africa and South America. The mould *Aspergillus flavus* was isolated from the meal, as was a toxin produced by the organism. The toxin was named *Aspergillus flavus* toxin – A-fla-toxin. It was later established that *Aspergillus parasiticus* also produces aflatoxins.

The production of aflatoxins occurs in a wide range of foods, including fresh beef, ham, bacon, milk, beer, cocoa, raisins and fermented sausage. Toxin production may occur within 4–10 days of contamination and growth. Circumstantial evidence suggests that aflatoxins are **carcinogenic** (*may* cause cancer) in humans.

Viruses

The role of viruses as agents of food poisoning is much less clearly understood. This is because viruses are cell parasites and cannot easily be grown in the laboratory. Some viruses cannot be grown in the laboratory at all. It is presumed that viruses, like bacteria, may be found in foods prepared in unhygienic conditions, although the viruses will not replicate in the food. It has been shown that virtually any food can act as a vehicle for virus transmission. The most common food source of viruses which cause gastro-intestinal illnesses are shellfish. In particular, filter feeders such as clams, mussels and oysters. There are many different types of viruses which can cause food-related illnesses, and of these Hepatitis A and the Norwalk viruses are particularly important.

There are more recorded incidents of Hepatitis A infection traced to food than any other viral infection. Children and young adults are particularly susceptible to infection. The incubation period ranges from 7–40 days and symptoms include anorexia, nausea, vomiting, fever, fatigue and gastrointestinal distress which are followed by the development of jaundice and accompanied by the swelling of the liver. This final phase may last several weeks and is sometimes accompanied by acute liver damage. The disease is fatal in less than 1% of cases, although this figure is variable. Death is more common in adults than children. Recovery is accompanied by the slow recovery of liver function and cell repair. Relapses are uncommon, although they have been reported. The return of full liver function takes about six months.

Infection is acquired orally, with common food vehicles being filter feeding shellfish, such as mussels grown in faecally contaminated water supplies. Whilst large explosive outbreaks do occur, particularly when water supplies are contaminated, the illness often occurs subclinically, i.e. the patient does not actually exhibit any symptoms although they are infected with the virus. As with other foodborne diseases these **asymptomatic carriers** can cause difficulties in controlling the spread of the virus.

Bacterial food poisoning

Bacteria are responsible for the vast majority of food poisoning cases reported. Food poisoning caused by bacteria can be divided into three categories, according to the mechanism of human infection. These groups are:

1   **Foodborne infections**   The illness is caused directly by the presence of the multiplying organisms in the intestines e.g. *Salmonella spp, Listeria monocytogenes.*

2   **Foodborne intoxications**   The illness is caused by a toxin produced by the micro-organism rather than by the presence of the organism itself. There are two possible routes to intoxication:

   a   the organisms grow in the food and thus produce a toxin; it may not matter whether the organisms are subsequently destroyed by cooking as some of the toxins are relatively heat stable and will still remain active. The key feature is the ingestion of food containing pre-formed toxin e.g. *Staphylococcus aureus, Clostridium botulinum.*

   b   the organisms produce the toxin, after ingestion, in the small intestine. In this case it is therefore necessary to ingest live organisms with the food e.g. *Vibrio parahaemolyticus, Escherichia coli, Clostridium perfringens.*

3   **Foodborne diseases**   The organisms do not grow in the food but simply use it as a vehicle to transfer them from host to host. These organisms fall into the category of infections that are caused via the **faecal-oral** route e.g. *Campylobacter jejuni, Salmonella typhi*. Other agents, such as the foodborne viruses, are also transmitted in this way.

The remainder of this chapter gives you information about some of the important food poisoning bacteria. It explores the incubation periods or onset time, the main symptoms and the duration of the illnesses.

Salmonella

Infections with salmonella account for the largest proportion of all reported outbreaks of food poisoning. This is because illness tends to occur amongst large groups of people, e.g. wedding receptions, hospitals, schools or amongst groups of individuals who have consumed common food items. In a small proportion of cases, individuals who have been ill and who have recovered

Salmonella (not *Salmonella typhi* or *Salmonella paratyphi*)	
Sources	Domestic animals including pets, human carriers, rodents, raw meats and poultry, raw eggs, raw milk. A wide range of processed foods have also been implicated in outbreaks of salmonellosis including salami sticks, chocolate, mayonnaise and cream cakes.
Incubation period	Between 6–72 hours, more usually 12–36 hours.
Symptoms & duration	Nausea, vomiting, abdominal pain, diarrhoea, fever. Usually lasts 2–3 days. May last longer particularly in the very old and the very young. Mortality about 4%. Some patients may become a **carrier** (see below).
Control	High standards of animal husbandry and the use of heat treated feeds. Refrigerated storage of all high risk foods. Thorough thawing of frozen meats and poultry. Prevention of cross contamination. High standards of personal and kitchen hygiene.

continue to excrete salmonella in their faeces. These individuals are called **convalescent carriers**. They may continue to excrete for several months and during that time must not handle food. Sometimes individuals may become infected with salmonella but do not develop illness. These individuals may excrete the organisms in their faeces too, and are called **healthy carriers**. Because these individuals cannot be identified, it is extremely important that all food handlers maintain extremely high standards of personal hygiene.

Clostridium perfringens

In catering operations, *Clostridium perfringens* poisoning is usually caused either by a failure to cool foods rapidly, or a failure to reheat food thoroughly. *Clostridium perfringens* are anaerobic bacteria which produce spores. The cooking of foods such as stews, gravies or large joints of meat drives the oxygen from the food, creating ideal conditions for the growth of the organism which is able to survive cooking by producing spores. During cooling the spores germinate and multiply rapidly.

Clostridium perfringens	
Sources	Commonly found in the soil, in dust, in faeces and raw meats.
Incubation period	8–12 hours.
Symptoms & duration	Abdominal pain, diarrhoea and nausea. Actual vomiting is rare. Usually lasts 12–48 hours.
Control	Illness is caused by the consumption of spores which germinate in the intestine. As these spores may survive cooking (see below) the main control methods are high standards of hygiene and the separation of raw and cooked foods.

Staphylococcus aureus

Staphylococcus aureus food poisoning is actually caused by a toxin produced by the organism as it grows in the food. It is the consumption of food containing this pre-formed toxin that makes you ill. The toxin is relatively heat stable and is unlikely to be destroyed by moderate cooking. The vast majority of outbreaks of *Staphylococcus aureus* food poisoning are caused by the direct contamination of food by food handlers.

Staphylococcus aureus	
Sources	Human skin, particularly the nose, mouth and throat. Also, infected spots and boils. May be found in associated with the skin of animals especially dairy cattle. Found in a wide range of foods.
Incubation period	1–6 hours.
Symptoms & duration	Severe abdominal cramps, vomiting which may be violent, lowering of the body temperature. Usually lasts 6–24 hours.
Control	Avoid handling food, high standards of personal hygiene. Exclusion of food handlers with infected wounds. Refrigeration of high risk foods.

Bacillus cereus

Bacillus cereus causes two types of food poisoning. This is due to the production of two toxins, one of which is produced in the food and one of which is produced in the intestines.

You will notice that the two illnesses caused by *Bacillus cereus* are different. The most common type in the UK is the vomiting illness. This is sometimes called 'Chinese fried-rice syndrome' because it often occurs after the consumption of take-away foods containing reheated rice.

Bacillus cereus		
Sources	Widely distributed throughout the environment, particularly in the soil and vegetation. The spores of these bacteria are commonly associated with rice and other cereal products.	
Incubation period	**Toxin in food** 1–5 hours.	**Toxin in intestines** 8–16 hours.
Symptoms & duration	Abdominal pain, **vomiting**, diarrhoea rare. Lasts 12–24 hours.	Abdominal pain, **diarrhoea**, vomiting rare. Lasts 24–48 hours.
Control	Thorough cooking and rapid cooling of foods.	

Clostridium botulinum

There are seven different types of *Clostridium botulinum*, A–G. Types A, B, E and F (rare) are associated with human food poisoning. Type E is **psychrotrophic** and is often associated with fish or fish products. *Clostridium botulinum* Type E can produce toxin at temperatures as low as 3.3°C, a good reason for ensuring the temperature of the chiller is low enough.

All types of *Clostridium botulinum* produce extremely heat resistant spores. Destruction of these spores is used to gauge the efficacy of the canning process. A temperature of 121°C for 3 minutes is used as the basis for their destruction in low acid canned foods. In foods where the pH is lower than 4.5, such strict controls are not necessary as toxin formation does not occur below this pH.

For human illness to occur, the spores must germinate and the organism multiply in the food, producing toxin as it grows. It is only consumption of food containing pre-formed toxin that will make us ill. Outbreaks of botulism are most often associated with the consumption of inadequately processed low-acid canned foods, or the consumption of contaminated fish (often smoked fish) products.

Clostridium botulinum	
Sources	Widely distributed in soil. Associated with fish, meats and vegetables.
Incubation period	2 hours–8 days. More usually between 12–36 hours.
Symptoms & duration	Progressive symptoms including difficulties in swallowing, slurred speech, dizziness, headache, muscle paralysis. Ultimately paralysis of the diaphragm which causes suffocation and death. Treatment with an antitoxin essential, recovery can take up to 2 years but more usually several months.
Control	Never use dented or damaged canned foods. Store smoked meat and fish products properly chilled or frozen. Ensure adequate cooking of raw foods.

EXERCISE

The most recent outbreak of botulism in the UK occurred in 1990 and was associated with the consumption of contaminated hazelnut yoghurt. This outbreak was interesting because of the reasons it happened. Find out about the outbreak from old newspapers and catering or food magazines, and work out why it happened (see O'Mahony *et al* (1990) in Useful Publications list, page 198).

Listeria monocytogenes

The reported incidence of listeriosis peaked in 1989. Whilst some of the reported cases may have been food-related, there is little direct evidence to support this claim. Surveys have shown that soft cheeses, pate, raw meats, ice-cream and chilled ready meals may contain *Listeria monocytogenes*.

Listeria monocytogenes	
Sources	Widely distributed in the natural environment and often isolated from river water, sewage and soils. Found in a wide range of foodstuffs including pate, ice-cream, sliced cooked meats and raw milk.
Incubation period	7 days–several weeks, depending upon the age and state of health of the infected individual.
Symptoms & duration	Depends upon the state of the individual infected; pregnant women may display influenza-like symptoms, may be symptomless or may abort. The foetus may be congenitally infected. Infants infected during delivery often develop meningitis. In susceptible non-pregnant adults, usually those with suppressed immune systems symptoms are typically meningitis and sepsis. AIDS, alcoholism, diabetes and cardiovascular disease are known to predispose adults to listeriosis. The mortality rate is about 28% amongst susceptible individuals.
Control	Prevention of cross-contamination. High standards of personal and kitchen hygiene. Use only pasteurised milk. Pregnant women should avoid unpastuerised dairy products and should thoroughly reheat chilled ready meals.

Other causes of foodborne infection and intoxication

The details given above do not provide a comprehensive list of all those bacteria which can cause foodborne infections and intoxications. As the varieties of foods we eat change, so do the types of micro-organism with which we come into contact. The micro-organisms also change, evolving to deal with the new food preservation technologies we have developed to slow their growth. For example, in recent years *Escherichia coli*, once a cause of illness usually only experienced by small children or those embarking on foreign travel, has become a serious cause for concern. *Escherichia coli* O157 H7 (a particular type of *E. coli*, also known as verocytotoxic *E. coli*) has become the cause of an increasing number of outbreaks of food-related illness amongst the elderly and the very young. In addition to the typical symptoms of vomiting and diarrhoea, it can cause kidney damage and ultimately kidney failure and death.

Foodborne diseases

Unlike the foodborne infections and intoxications, most foodborne diseases occur relatively rarely in this country. This is due to several factors, notably the provision of a safe supply of drinking water and generally high standards of personal hygiene. The organisms which cause these illnesses are transmitted by the faecal oral route (Figure 31). The organism or agent of infection is transported by the food which acts only as a vehicle of transmission rather than

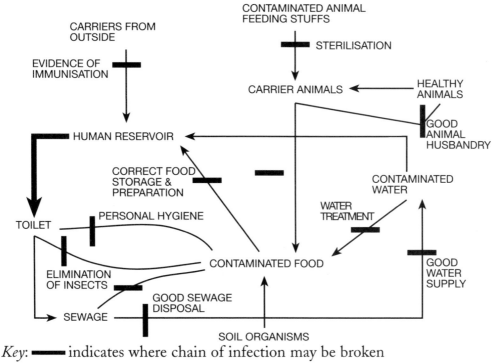

Key: ▬▬ indicates where chain of infection may be broken
Figure 31: The faecal oral route

a medium for multiplication. The bacteria which cause typhoid fever, dysentery, brucellosis, tuberculosis and campylobacter enteritis are examined here. Hepatitis A also falls into this category but is considered briefly above.

Typhoid

Typhoid and paratyphoid fevers are caused respectively by *Salmonella typhi* and *Salmonella paratyhphi*.

Typhoid fever was for a long time one of the most common and widespread of all bacterial diseases. However, its prevalence has greatly diminished, particularly in the developed countries. In the less developed parts of the world or in areas with poor sanitation and large numbers of people, notably refugee camps, it is still common.

Sometimes considered primarily to be an intestinal infection, typhoid fever is in fact a general body infection. The gastrointestinal tract is generally the route of entry of the organism to the body, i.e. the organisms enter the body via the mouth (faecal-oral route). The infective dose is very small. It is this excretion of

Typhoid and paratyphoid fevers	
Source	Both *Salmonella typhi* and *Salmonella paratyphi* infect only humans and are transmitted from human host to human host via the faecal oral route.
Incubation period	Usually between 1–3 weeks.
Symptoms & duration	The symptoms of typhoid fever include headache, fatigue, bronchitis, high fever and abdominal tenderness with diarrhoea being uncommon at this stage. After a few days clinically typical 'rose spots' appear in the skin. Relapses are common. The illness may last several weeks. The symptoms of paratyphoid fever are similar but less severe than those of typhoid fever.
Control	Eliminate the source of infection, particularly through the control of carriers. Prevent the spread of infection by public health measures, safe disposal of sewage, clean water supply, hygienic preparation of food and most significantly immunisation.

organisms that perpetuates the cycle, i.e. via the consumption of organisms in food, from hands etc. contaminated by organisms of a diseased individual or of a carrier. Between 2–5% of cases still excrete the organism up to one year after the infection, while some individuals excrete for life. Nearly all permanent excreters are women.

Dysentery

Dysentery can be caused by infection by a range of organisms, notably bacteria of the genus *Shigella* (bacillary dysentery), protozoa (amoebic dysentery) and indeed many viruses. Most commonly however it is the bacterial form that is diagnosed. Bacillary dysentery is acquired by mouth, the source of organisms being faecal, from a case or carrier. Individuals with mild or symptomless infections outnumber those with symptoms and constitute the main reservoir of infection. Patients recovering from dysentery may excrete the organisms for several weeks after recovery but permanent carriers are rare. In tropical countries, epidemics are associated with low standards of hygiene, with flies being an important vector in transferring the organisms from faeces to food. In the UK, the rare cases which occur are often due to faecal contamination of crockery, door handles, lavatory chains and seats. The organisms may also be conveyed by food contaminated by a carrier.

Amoebic dysentery is caused by the protozoan *Entamoeba histolytica* which lives in the human intestinal tract. It burrows into the lining of the large intestine and damages the underlying tissues, producing localised swelling. In some cases the amoebae gain access to the blood stream and produce hepatitis or liver abscesses. Amoebic dysentery mainly occurs in tropical and subtropical

Dysentery	
Sources	Faecal-oral transmission via infected individuals, food and water. No animal reservoir of infection is known.
Incubation period	For bacillary dysentery between 1–7 days.
Symptoms	Ranging from minor bowel discomfort to diarrhoea with or without blood and mucous. In severe cases intestinal tissue damage may occur.
Control	Eliminate the source of infection, particularly through the control of carriers. Prevent the spread of infection by public health measures, safe disposal of sewage, clean water supply, hygienic preparation of food.

countries, and it generally lasts longer than bacillary dysentery. Acute attacks of diarrhoea sometimes occur but it is more normal for the patient to produce three or four bulky stools each day. The disease will persist and become chronic if untreated, in which case the amoebae tend to encyst (i.e. will produce cysts). Cysts are protective mechanisms which allow the organisms to survive for very long periods. Such cysts may be excreted in the faeces for many years. Amoebic dysentery is transmitted by the ingestion of cysts in contaminated foods, particularly raw vegetables fruit and water. The use of human faeces as a fertiliser is responsible for the heavy infestation in some areas.

Brucellosis

Organisms of the genus *Brucella* are primarily animal pathogens, and humans become infected as the result of contact with infected animals. In cows and goats, brucellae are responsible for abortion and may be excreted in milk for long periods. They are also excreted in faeces and urine. Human infections are generally found amongst farmers, veterinary surgeons and individuals working with infected animals. The organisms gain access via skin abrasions, through the alimentary tract and possibly through the respiratory tract. In the general population, infection is almost inevitably the direct result of contaminated unpasteurised milk. The disease is becoming increasingly less common due to the compulsory pasteurisation of milk.

Brucellosis	
Source	Farm animals such as cattle, sheep, goats and pigs. Consumption of contaminated raw milk or milk products.
Incubation period	Usually 5–21 days.
Symptoms	An intermittent fever, headache, weakness and generalised body aching which may last from a few days to many months.
Control	Compulsory pasteurisation of milk, and compulsory slaughter of infected animals.

Tuberculosis

Human tuberculosis is generally caused by *Mycobacterium tuberculosis*. *Mycobacterium bovis* causes tuberculosis in cattle, and is sometimes transmitted to humans. Immunisation and the slaughter of infected animals means that this disease is now rare in cattle. The incidence in humans is increasing, particularly amongst those living 'rough'.

Tuberculosis (*Mycobacterium tuberculosis*)	
Sources	Droplet and airborne transmission, contact with infected sputum. Bovine TB is primarily spread by the consumption of raw milk and dairy products
Incubation period	Between 4–6 weeks, although the more serious later stages of the disease may take years to develop.
Symptoms	Lung congestion and night sweats are common, and a failure of wounds to heal properly. As the disease progresses, clusters of the micro-organisms (tubercules) settle in the body (anywhere though often in bone) where they cause further damage.
Control	Bovine TB is controlled by the compulsory slaughter of infected animals. Milkborne TB is controlled by compulsory heat treatment of milk. Adequate housing and hygienic living conditions control TB amongst the general population.

Campylobacter

Campylobacter was confirmed as a cause of human enteritis in 1977. Since then it has been identified as the cause of illness in an increasing number of reported cases. In 1991 campylobacter was established as the cause of illness in 32,636 cases. In most of these cases, the food vehicle was not identified. This is because the cases tend to be **sporadic** (occurring as single unrelated incidents rather than in **outbreaks**). The number of reported cases peaks in late spring with young adults (roughly between the ages of 20–30) being most susceptible. Of these, males tend to be more susceptible than females, although the reasons for this are unclear (see table overleaf).

Campylobacter jejuni	
Sources	Commonly found in the intestinal tract of farm animals, poultry and in farm wastes. The organisms are also found in sewage and river water. Common food vehicles include poultry, raw milk, bottled milk pecked by birds, offal, beef, pork and lamb.
Incubation period	Highly variable; usually 48–82 hours but may be as long as 7–10 days or more.
Symptoms & duration	Abdominal pain, diarrhoea, headache, fever. Usually lasting between 1–4 days. In severe cases blood is associated with diarrhoea. The organisms may be excreted in faeces for up to 2 months after recovery from the illness.
Control	Pasteurisation of milk. Prevention of cross contamination. Thorough cooking of meats. Hygiene training of food handlers and increasing awareness amongst consumers.

EXERCISE

The following exercises require you to read about some outbreaks of food-mediated disease and to answer questions about the outbreaks. The first three cases are short, while the fourth is a more involved exercise based around the notorious outbreak of salmonellosis that occurred at Stanley Royd Hospital in August 1984.

The following case studies have been adapted from real outbreaks of food poisoning. Using your knowledge of the bacterial causes of food poisoning, answer the questions after each case study.

Food poisoning at a picnic

A caterer baked 14 large hams in an oven from 2100–0645h the next day. Internal temperatures were reported to have reached 74°C. The hams were boned by hand and were sliced by two teenage men whilst still warm. The slices of ham were stacked into several large gastronome trays, covered with aluminium foil and put in the back of the oven at about 0800h with the thermostat set at 93°C.

At 1400h the pans of sliced ham were taken by car to the picnic site were they remained until required at 1800h. A person who ate some ham when it arrived became ill one and a half hours before the main meal was served – no connection was made between the illness and the ham at the time.

Within four hours of eating the ham, 244 of the picnickers were showing signs of food poisoning (particularly violent vomiting and stomach cramps), and 120 needed hospital treatment.

Staphylococcus aureus was isolated from the ham and from the hands and from a boil on the face of one of the food handlers who sliced the ham.

◆ Outline step by step the sequence of events that led to this outbreak of food poisoning.
◆ What steps need to be taken to ensure that such an outbreak does not happen again?

Food poisoning at a prison

At least 42 inmates of a prison developed the symptoms of nausea, vomiting, stomach pains and diarrhoea between one and a half, and three hours after eating a meal of beef stew, mashed potatoes and peas. Accurate case histories were not obtained but most patients appeared to have developed symptoms of nausea and vomiting; less than half reported diarrhoea and associated abdominal pain. In most cases the symptoms lasted less than 12 hours and the following morning only nine inmates reported ill.

The beef dish was cooked in a steam heated boiling pan along with the vegetables which were pre-cooked that morning and had been left at ambient temperature in the kitchen until mealtime. An unverified report indicated that the previous day's leftover vegetables were also added to bulk out the meal. This mixture was cooked for about one hour, although a simmering temperature was not maintained throughout this period. About 200 inmates were served the stew; about 175 detected a 'sour' smell and did not eat it: none of these inmates were ill.

Four faecal samples were submitted for examination as was a portion of the incriminated stew. Micro-organisms were present in large numbers in the stew, as was the toxin of the implicated organism.

◆ Which of the common causes of food poisoning is likely to have been the cause of this outbreak? Give reasons for your answer.

Food preparation at a home for the elderly

I witnessed the following sequence of events at a home for the elderly. I declined the invitation to lunch; would you?

On a hot sunny day in July, the cook at a residential home for the elderly (38 residents, some very ill) was preparing lunch for both residents and staff. The menu was boiled gammon with parsley sauce and vegetables, followed by pineapple upside-down-cake and custard.

The gammon had been soaked and boiled the previous day. It had been put into a pan and placed in the refrigerator overnight. The refrigerator was operating at a temperature of 11°C. At 0900h the cook took the gammon from the refrigerator and sliced it on a dirty slicing machine. The sliced meat was placed into aluminium trays, covered with metal foil and placed on the side at ambient temperature until required for lunch at noon.

Next the cook prepared the vegetables to accompany the main course and then he made the parsley sauce and the custard. Both the parsley sauce and the custard were left in uncovered saucepans on the top of the stove. He then made the pineapple upside-down-cake and put it into the oven to bake. By now it was 1030h; the cook went to the toilet and found that he could not wash his hands because the kitchen assistant had filled the hand wash basin with dirty utensils. He made a pot of tea and prepared a plate of biscuits and called his colleague the gardener into the kitchen for a cup of tea.

The gardener came into the kitchen and using his dirty finger tasted both the parsley sauce and the custard. Having pronounced himself satisfied with these components of his lunch, he had a cup of tea. Whilst the colleagues were drinking their tea a magpie came to the

EXERCISE

open kitchen door. The cook took some of the cooked gammon and hand fed it to the bird, a frequent visitor to the kitchen. After finishing their tea the gardener went to the toilet and on his way outside through the kitchen again tasted the contents of the two pans.

The cook finished off the lunch. He heated the hot cupboard so that the dial read 70°C and at 1130h he put the plates and the sliced gammon into the cupboard. Lunch was served at 1200h to all patients and staff. After the main course the cook served the pineapple upside-down-cake and custard which he only partially reheated as 'the residents don't like it too hot'.

◆ Would an outbreak of food poisoning from this sequence of events surprise you? Give reasons.
◆ Which food poisoning organisms could find their way into this food preparation chain?

To complete this last, more detailed exercise you will need to read:

The Report Of The Committee Of Inquiry Into An Outbreak Of Food Poisoning At Stanley Royd Hospital (1986) HMSO, London.

Read the case study and then answer the following questions:

1   Produce a brief synopsis which clearly describes the sequence of events that occurred at Stanley Royd Hospital between 26 August–11 September 1984.

2   The Report of the Committee of Inquiry identified the 'basic cause of the outbreak' as human error. However, the Report also states '. . . it is much easier to be hygienic in a kitchen which is itself hygienic . . .' p 69 para 204).

    a Describe conditions in the Stanley Royd kitchens at the time of the outbreak.

    b What measures would you recommend to improve this situation?

EXERCISE

c What implications does this report have for you as a future manager in the catering industry?

3   Use your library to find out how the newspapers reported this outbreak. How does this compare to the reporting of more recent outbreaks of food poisoning?

Food Hygiene and You

Illness caused by eating food does not happen by itself. If an outbreak does occur there is always a single common factor: the food handler. Research in both the UK and USA has shown that of the 'top ten' factors implicated in outbreaks of food-mediated disease, the most common linking factor is people. However small your involvement with food in a catering operation, you have a legal and a moral responsibility to practise the highest standards of personal hygiene. The Food Safety (General Food Hygiene) Regulations 1995 identify key areas which you are required to observe (see Chapter 5, page 73). A failure to do so renders you liable to prosecution and fines of up to £2000 per offence identified. This chapter outlines the most important areas of personal hygiene.

By the end of this chapter you should be able to
- list the reasons why personal hygiene is important to the food handler
- explain why protective clothing is worn
- explain why food handlers must be excluded from food handling if they acquire certain illnesses

YOUR BODY'S MICROBIOLOGY

Your body is an important source of micro-organisms. Your skin is home to many different types of bacteria which live on its surface or in the pores. This is one reason why our sweat smells. Your mouth too has its own population of bacteria, and these organisms are responsible for dental caries and for the smell of bad breath. Your intestinal tract contains various types of micro-organisms down its entire length. These organisms are important in the digestion of some foods and even produce some vitamins for us to use.

YOU THE FOOD HANDLER

In order that we maintain high standards of personal hygiene it is essential that we wash regularly and change and launder our clothes frequently. It is important that food handlers are aware that their body is a source of micro-organisms.

Your hands

Your hands are potentially the most dangerous implement with which you may handle food. They naturally carry bacteria on their surface and may acquire pathogens and spoilage organisms from raw foods, after visits to the toilet, or from other parts of your body unless you are very careful. Your hands are likely to harbour most bacteria, on or under your nails or jewellery. That is why it is forbidden to wear most items of jewellery when handling food. You can reduce the numbers of organisms on your hands by following the following basic rules:

1   Keep your hands visibly clean – wash your hands frequently and don't let dirt and stains accumulate.

2   Ensure your nails are kept short and clean – the wearing of nail varnish is prohibited because it can chip and flake into food. It also makes it difficult to see how clean your nails are. Use a nail brush to ensure you remove as much dirt as possible.

3   Jewellery, with the exception of a plain wedding band, is not permitted as it may fall off into food. Patterned or jewelled rings are not allowed as they can accumulate large numbers of organisms. Watches, bangles and leather or cotton bracelets are a particular hazard and are not permitted.

4   Wash your hands thoroughly and regularly using a bactericidal soap and hot water. Dry your hands thoroughly using disposable paper towels or hot air dryers. Fabric hand towels accumulate dirt and moisture and should be avoided. Always wash your hands:

- after using the toilet
- after combing your hair
- after sneezing or blowing your nose
- after handling raw food
- after handling waste
- before handling cooked food
- on entering the kitchen
- after a break.

Your hair

Your hair is constantly falling out and may contaminate food directly. It also often carries *Staphylococcus aureus* which can cause food poisoning (see Chapter

8, page 139). Your hair may therefore cause physical and biological contamination simultaneously. Dandruff can also contaminate food and for these reasons all food handlers must wear an appropriate head covering. Beards too must be covered with a suitable mask or beard net.

You must not comb your hair whilst you are wearing protective clothing as any loose hairs which fall onto the clothing may subsequently fall into food. You should shampoo your hair regularly as this helps to reduce the numbers of organisms on the scalp. The use of fashionable hair ornaments should be avoided and any grips or combs that are worn must be secured under the protective head covering to prevent them from falling into food. Individuals with head sores should not be permitted to handle food.

Your ears, nose and mouth

The nose, mouth and ears are frequently contaminated by *Staphylococcus aureus* and other bacteria. These bacteria can be transmitted to food by coughing, sneezing, spitting, by hand contact (e.g. picking nose or ears). Ear rings, nose rings and other facial jewellery must not be worn as they may fall out and contaminate food.

Food handlers must not smoke, spit, take snuff or indulge in other habits which may cause them to cough or sneeze. Hand to mouth contact should be avoided as it assist the transfer of bacteria. This means that food handlers should not dip their fingers into food to taste it, lick their fingers to open plastic bags or eat in a food preparation area. Individuals who are suffering from bad colds or flu should not be permitted to handle food for the same reasons.

Other parts of your body

Any part of the body which may come into contact with food should be adequately covered and protected. This may include the forearms and neck, particularly for butchers who may have to lift heavy meat carcasses. Facial cosmetics should not be used as they may flake into food or may cause irritation to the eyes initiating hand to face contact. Perfume may taint food and should therefore not be used. The use of scented soaps, creams and body sprays should also be limited. Food service staff should consider these points and apply make-up in moderation.

SELF-CHECK QUESTIONS

---

1   *When must you wash your hands if you are handling food?*
2   *How can your hair contaminate food?*
3   *Which common food poisoning bacteria lives on your skin?*

General illness

All food handlers have a legal responsibility to report to their superiors if they may be suffering from any illness which might cause contamination of foodstuffs and lead to food mediated illness. If you, or anyone else in your household develops the symptoms of food poisoning, you must not handle food and should be excluded from these duties until you are cleared by your doctor and are fit to work.

If during or after a holiday abroad you develop these symptoms, you must also notify your superiors and not resume food handling duties until you have obtained medical clearance.

The Food Safety (General Food Hygiene) Regulations 1995 state that food handlers who suspect that they may be suffering from a disease which is likely to be transmitted through food, *must* tell their superior and should not handle food. Handlers should also notify their superiors if:

◆ they have a skin infection or an infected wound
◆ they suspect that as the result of an earlier illness, they may be the carrier of a disease which could be transmitted through food.

Whilst the Food Safety (General Food Hygiene) Regulations 1995 do not specify particular illnesses which fall into the categories outlined, it is appropriate to consider that these remain unchanged from previous legislation (Table 17).

◆ Salmonella infections including typhoid fever and paratyphoid fever
◆ Viral gastroenteritis
◆ Hepatitis A
◆ Food poisoning
◆ Infected skin wounds or boils
◆ Parasitic infections including illnesses caused by *Giardia* and *Cryptosporidium*
◆ *Escherichia coli* infections

Table 17: Illnesses for which food handlers may be excluded from work

Protective clothing for food handlers

Your outdoor clothes will be contaminated with a wide range of micro-organisms, dirt and dust from the environment. Your shoes in particular may carry the remains of faecal material from the pavements or soil. It is particularly important that none of these things are allowed to contaminate food and it is for this reason that you must wear protective clothing when handling food. Your protective clothing should consist of:

Overalls

Your overalls or kitchen whites must either cover or completely replace your outdoor clothes. They must be light in colour, preferably white so that it is easy to see when they are dirty. Your overalls must not be torn or tattered around the edges, as frayed fabric can fall into food. In addition, it looks untidy and is not appealing to your customers.

All fastenings must be adequately secured to the garment as they could cause a contamination risk. Always check your overalls carefully after they have been laundered.

Aprons

You should wear an apron in addition to your whites for dirty tasks or where additional protection is required. The apron must again be light in colour and for some jobs it may be appropriate that it is waterproof. Disposable aprons are available and are generally made of plastic. They should be pale blue rather than white so that they can be seen if they contaminate food. Non-disposable aprons should be resistant to continuous washing as they will need to washed after each use.

Hats and head coverings

Hats should completely cover the head. The traditional chef's stove hat should be worn with an accompanying hair net to cover the hair completely. Hair nets must be made of a mesh which has holes but will not allow hair ornaments and grips to fall out. They should be white so that it can be seen when they are dirty. Hats and hair nets are equally important for men and women.

Gloves

These may be required for certain operations. It should be remembered that gloves do not prevent your hands contaminating food; only good kitchen practices can do that. For operations where you need to wear gloves, they should be made of an appropriate material and be light in colour.

Footwear

Non-slip, robust shoes with welded uppers should be worn as they provide protection from falling objects knives etc. Shoes should be waterproof, comfortable and must be restricted for use in the food environment. For wet areas, rubber boots with non-slip soles are easy to keep clean and disinfect.

General appearance

You are likely to be asked about your general state of health if you apply for a job handling food. When you attend for interview you can expect to be inspected for high standards of personal hygiene. A clean, neat appearance indicates to the potential employer that you have the right attitude to your work. This is important as customers are put off by staff with a poor attitude to personal hygiene.

SELF CHECK QUESTIONS

I   *Under what circumstances should food handlers not be allowed to handle food?*

2   *Itemise the different types of protective clothing that a food handler should wear.*

EXERCISES

Two exercises are presented here. The first is an observation exercise that does not require any special equipment or facilities, and the second is a practical exercise that should only be undertaken in a microbiology laboratory.

1   Observations

Having read this section of the book you should now understand why high standards of personal hygiene are so important for food handlers. To investigate personal hygiene amongst food handlers, draw up a checklist of all the key points that relate to dress, work practices, hand washing practices etc. Spend time observing how personal hygiene is managed in the kitchen and other key areas of the work environment e.g. toilets, rest rooms, changing rooms. This exercise can also be used in conjunction with the kitchen practices exercise in the next chapter.

2   Practical: The recovery of *S. aureus* and other micro-organisms from your skin

Your body (both inside and out) provides a perfect home for many different types of micro-organisms; your gut harbours millions of microbes which are essential to your health and well being. Your skin and hair also provide an ideal home for many different types of micro-

EXERCISES

organisms. The types and numbers of organisms are affected by the clothes, the types of deodorants, perfumes, make-up, jewellery etc. we wear. As we have seen in this chapter there is one particular skin micro-organism which is of particular significance in relation to food hygiene, *Staphylococcus aureus*. It is partly due to the presence of this organism that the maintenance of high standards of personal hygiene is so important for food handlers. In this exercise you will find out whether you carry *S. aureus* on your skin and examine some of the other micro-organisms that live on some of the more accessible parts of your body, on your clothes and on your head.

Skin

The following method will enable you to find out whether you carry *S aureus* on your skin.

Take a Baird-Parker Agar (Oxoid) plate. Label the base with your name, class and for incubation at 37°C. Draw a line dividing the plate in half with a marker pen. Place your fingers gently onto one half of the agar so that you leave faint fingerprints. On the other half of the plate, using a sterile swab moistened with sterile diluent (I suggest $^{1}/_{4}$ strength Ringers-Oxoid), wipe gently and carefully around the inside edge of your nostril, streak over the second half of the plate in a zig zag fashion. Incubate the plates for 48 hours at 37°C.

After incubation, the presence of *Staphylococcus aureus* is indicated by the presence of shiny, black, convex colonies, 2–4mm diameter, surrounded by a zone of clearing in the agar giving the colony a haloed appearance. Record the results for your group in a table.

Compare your results with the rest of the group. What proportion of the group are *Staphylococcus aureus* carriers

<u>a</u>   in the nose; and

<u>b</u>   on the hands?

How do these figures compare with statistics for the entire population? Your results may vary from this figure; why might this be? Discuss your findings with other members of your group.

EXERCISES

Other micro-organisms also live quite naturally on our skin. By using the methods detailed here you can examine some of these organisms.

Hair and ears

Using a Nutrient Agar (Oxoid) plate, label and divide the plate as before. This time place a hair pulled carefully from your head on one half; on the other, again using a swab moistened in Ringers, swab behind your ear and then streak the plate. Incubate aerobically for 24 hours at 37°C. If you have the facilities repeat this procedure using a Reinforced Clostridial Agar (Oxoid) plate which should then be incubated anaerobically at 37°C for 24 hours.

After incubation compare the pattern of growth on the two plates.

Organisms of the same type produce identical colonies. By looking carefully at the size, shape, colour and surface texture of the colonies which have grown, you should be able to estimate the number and variety of organisms which have grown on your plate.

Have the same organisms grown on each plate? What are the possible reasons for your findings? Is this what you expected to find? Explain your answers.

Hands

The types of micro-organisms on our hands tend to reflect what we've been doing! It is therefore important to ensure that we wash our hands thoroughly before we handle food. Watches, rings and other jewellery can also harbour bacteria, which is why we must remove them before we handle food.

Using a Nutrient Agar (Oxoid) plate, divided in half as before, make fingerprints on one half. On the other half either swab behind a watch strap or inside a ring and streak onto the plate. Incubate these plates at 37°C for 24 hours. After incubation examine the plates to see what has grown. What implications do these results have on your behaviour in the kitchen?

Clothes

In the kitchen environment you are expected to wear 'whites' but have you ever thought of the reason why? Not only to protect you from spillages etc., but also to protect the food from contamination from your outdoor clothes.

Using a Nutrient Agar (Oxoid) contact plate press it firmly to a shirt/blouse which is next to your skin. Hold the plate in contact with the garment for 15 seconds. Label the plate to indicate which garment you sampled and then incubate at 30°C for 48 hours. After incubation examine the plate to see what has grown.
Are there as many organisms or as many different types of organisms as you expected? What may be the reasons for your results? How do your results compare with other members of your group?

Food Hygiene in the Kitchen

In previous chapters you have learned how food handling practices and food handlers themselves can contaminate food. In order that food is protected from contamination, it is necessary that the high standards of hygiene you have already learned about are complemented by well designed and laid out premises which are easy to maintain and clean. This minimises the risks of pest infestations. This chapter examines the basic principles of premises design and kitchen layout necessary to facilitate good hygiene, the importance of cleaning and disinfection in food premises and the problems associated with pest control.

DESIGN, CONSTRUCTION AND LAYOUT OF PREMISES

By the end of this section you should be able to
- list the services required by a catering operation
- describe the main structural features necessary in a well planned catering operation

What constitute food premises?

The Food Safety Act 1990 defines food premises as anywhere food is prepared, stored or sold; this includes farms, shops, restaurants, market stalls, food processing factories, ships and aeroplanes. With very few exceptions, all food premises must be registered with the Local Authority (Food Premises (Registration) Regulations 1991). The exceptions are those businesses that operate for less than five days in a five week period.

Choosing the site of a new food business

Whether the new business will operate from a purpose built building on a green field site or from an existing converted premises, it is necessary that the following basic points are considered:

Provision and availability of services

All mains services should be available e.g. electricity, gas and telephone. Water provision must be via a potable mains supply and effluent disposal should be via mains drainage, not septic tank. This is unlikely to be a problem for existing buildings but may have more serious implications for construction on a green field site.

Accessibility

The site should be readily accessible for the delivery of raw materials and for the distribution of the final product. When choosing the site, care should be taken to ensure that staff will be able to reach the building easily using public transport. This is particularly important for food businesses that operate 24 hour shifts.

Flooding

The proximity of rivers and the height of water table (at flood) should also be considered, as it is not acceptable to prepare food in an environment contaminated by flood water. Again this is more significant when selecting a green field site, but it should be noted that very high tides and seasonal storms can lead to flooding in some areas not previously thought at risk. Such events are likely to raise insurance premiums which could have a direct impact on the viability of a business and should therefore be investigated at the planning stage.

Unacceptable contamination

Care must be taken to ensure that contamination from chemicals, dust, odour pests etc. is not likely. For example, it is not acceptable to site a food operation downwind of a sewage treatment works or a cement works, both of which would be likely to cause contamination of the food.

Pollution caused by operation

Whilst it is important to consider the impact of the environment on the food operation, it is essential to consider the impact of the food business on the local environment. Food operations can generate a lot of noise, e.g. from noisy machinery, often at antisocial hours. Shift working, the unloading and loading of goods may also lead to complaints.

It is appropriate that these features are carefully considered prior to any application for planning permission. Once outline planning permission has been granted, it is necessary to design the interior of the premises with care. This requires consultation between those operating the business, the local Environmental Health Officers, architects and planners. The aim should be to design and build a building which:

- provides adequate workspace
- facilitates linear production flow
- facilitates adequate cleaning
- eliminates cross-contamination
- allows for profitable production and possible expansion.

If the premises are being refitted rather than built from scratch, there will undoubtedly be limiting factors, such as inconveniently situated supporting walls that cannot be removed, or limited space impeding linear flow. These problems can usually be overcome with care.

The building

As with all the features considered during the site selection process, many of the features described here are more relevant to a new building rather than an existing one. However, the basic principles should be considered when selecting a building for conversion into a food production operation of any sort.

The building's foundations and all external walls should be water, rodent and insect proof. All points where piping or ducting enters or exits a building, and all doorways and windows, should be adequately proofed to prevent access by pests. The area surrounding the building should as far as possible be clear of debris and plant cover. This reduces the likelihood of pests gaining access to the building as it denies them cover in the immediate vicinity of the building. In cities where terraced buildings are occupied by restaurants, care should be taken to reduce the accumulation of waste around the rear and the accessibility of the building for the same reasons.

The integrity and structural design of the roof should also be considered. In a new building, great care should be taken not to provide roosting sites for birds. Care should also be taken to avoid pooling of water which will also attract birds to the site. In old, existing buildings, roosting birds can be both a noise and public health nuisance if not controlled properly.

Ceilings and overhead fittings

Ceilings may either be suspended or solid. Suspended ceilings conceal pipework and main service cables but must be fitted with inspection hatches to facilitate maintenance access, cleaning and pest control. Solid ceilings provide less scope for a hygienic finish as pipework and service cables protrude. They must be well insulated to prevent condensation and mould growth.

Whatever the construction of the ceilings they should have a smooth finish, be light in colour and easy to clean. The height of the ceiling may be pre-determined in an old building, but it should be sufficient to provide a good quality working environment rather than a claustrophobic environment.

Lighting should be of a high standard to produce a safe working environment. Good lighting also makes cleaning easier and is less stressful for employees. Lighting provision must comply with legislation which states that all fixtures must be captive and positioned so that no part can fall or shatter onto or into food materials. Artificial lighting is preferred to natural light (sunlight) as it reduces glare and heat gain caused by bright sunlight. Fluorescent tubes fitted with diffusers are recommended.

Walls

Internal wall surfaces should have a smooth, impervious finish and be free from cracks and crevices where pests, food and debris may lodge. They should be constructed of durable materials, with the provision of additional protection against impact where necessary; e.g. if fork lift trucks or stacking trolleys are routinely used.

Walls should be light in colour, and finished with an impervious and non-flaking material. Both painted and non-painted walls may be susceptible to damage by cleaning chemicals and micro-organisms (particularly moulds).

The junctions between walls and floors, and walls and ceilings should be sealed and rounded for easy cleaning. To prevent easy access for pests, solid walls are preferred to those with cavities. Pipework must be sealed as it enters and exits through the walls, and doors should be tight fitting and self-closing.

Floors and drainage

The general properties of floors are similar to those of walls, but floors must be finished so that they are resistant to the effects of grease and cleaning agents. They must also be non-slip, which is particularly important in food operations where steam is produced and water spillages are common. Floors must also be easy to clean. As cleaning often uses large volumes of water, it is advisable that the floor slopes slightly towards a drainage point. This avoids the pooling of water which is not only a safety hazard but may also provide an excellent growth medium for bacteria.

When selecting a floor covering, the following points should be considered:

◆ the volume and nature of traffic, i.e. is the floor used by trolleys and fork lift trucks as well as people?
◆ is it a wet or dry area?
◆ how is cleaning carried out?
◆ is chemical resistance necessary?
◆ can production continue if repairs need to be made?

All drains must be able to cope with peak load without flooding back into the kitchen. They must be clean, cleanable and easy to maintain. It is therefore best to avoid a totally covered system. Drains should be fitted with traps to collect solid materials (grease traps if necessary) and with water locks to avoid odour in food areas. Inspection access should, where possible, be outside food rooms, but if access points in the kitchen area are unavoidable, air-tight covers should be fitted. Potato peelers, dishwashers, and waste disposal units which may be plumbed directly into mains drainage, should be fitted with traps to avoid blockage by waste and water locks to avoid odour.

Ventilation

Adequate ventilation is essential in a kitchen, to reduce the humidity and temperatures which may facilitate growth of moulds and other micro-organisms. The quality of the final product may also be affected by poor environmental air quality in the production area.

Fitting out a food business

The construction of the food business determines how easily it can be maintained and cleaned. A food business which is appropriately laid out and equipped, clean and well maintained in turn creates a quality working environment. In addition to consideration of the fabric of the building, work flow and utilisation of available space are also important features of a well designed food operation.

Work flow and utilisation of space

Work flow should separate clean processes from dirty thus preventing cross-contamination. This can be done using physical barriers such as walls or by imposing a single direction on product flow (see Figure 32). In practice the former method is more commonly used as sufficient space and equipment to permit linear flow are rarely available.

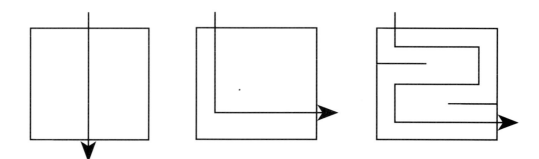

Figure 32: The utilisation of space to facilitate linear work flow

In any kitchen there is likely to be some overlap of processes and personnel which could create the opportunity for cross contamination to occur. This may occur when dirty utensils and equipment are taken to the pot wash from all areas of a kitchen on a single trolley and are similarly returned. Or it could occur when personnel move from one area to another to undertake various tasks.

SELF CHECK QUESTIONS

1   *What main services must be available for a catering operation?*
2   *What are the main structural features which should be considered when planning a catering operation?*

PEST CONTROL IN THE KITCHEN

By the end of this section you should be able to
- explain what is meant by the term food pest
- list the main types of food pest
- describe the likely signs of pest infestation
- describe the main means of controlling food pests

One of the main reasons for the care needed with building structure is to avoid the infestation of the premises with potential food pests. A food pest is an animal, insect or bird which lives on or in food and causes damage or contamination of the product. Many food businesses are closed every year as a direct result of pest infestations, and many thousands of pounds worth of food are destroyed with thousands more spent on pesticides. It is essential that pests are kept out of a food business and that if they do gain access they are eliminated rapidly and thoroughly.

The common food pests include:

◆ rodents: rats and mice
◆ insects: flies, wasps and ants, cockroaches, psocids (booklice), silverfish and a whole range of stored product insects including flour beetles and weevils
◆ birds: mainly feral pigeons and sparrows.

Rodents

There are three rodents which cause problems in food businesses: the brown or

Norway rat (*Rattus norvegicus*), the black or ship rat (*Rattus rattus*) and the house mouse (*Mus domesticus*).

The black rat

The black rat enters this country from ships and other freight ports. Its distribution tends to be confined to relatively small areas around these points of entry. It is an excellent climber and may be found in the roofs and upper storeys of buildings. It is omnivorous but prefers fruit and vegetables. It is a slender animal with a pointed nose and large mouse-like ears. The tail is longer than the combined length of the head and body.

The brown rat

The brown rat is found all over the UK. It is larger than the black rat, lighter in colour and has a blunt nose and small ears. It is an excellent swimmer and is frequently found in sewers or along riverbanks and canals where it lives in burrows. It is also omnivorous but prefers cereal foods.

The house mouse

The house mouse enters buildings seeking warmth, particularly in cold weather. Mice forage for food over a relatively small area, nibbling both food and non-food items as they move. They prefer cereal foods but will spoil a wide variety of products. The house mouse is small with a pointed head and large ears. It has a very long tail and imparts a characteristic smell to its nests. These animals are very successful at cohabiting with man and as they breed rapidly, they can cause significant damage if allowed to infest a food business.

Signs of rodent infestation

Rodents leave droppings and urine smears at feeding points. Brown rats may mark favoured runs with fur and urine. All rodents need to gnaw at hard items to grind their teeth, so table legs, packaging, electric flexes etc. may show teeth marks. Sitings of live animals and finding dead bodies are also likely signs of infestation.

Control of rodent infestation

Tracking powders may be used to establish the nature of the infestation followed by the use of baits or traps. Baits contain an attractive food combined with a rodenticide (rodent poison). Baits are usually placed into boxes so they are less hazardous to personnel. They also provide cover for the feeding animal. Traps may be used to identify the infesting animal species, to trap individuals or if there is a risk of contaminating food. The advantage of using traps is that they prevent animals dying in inaccessible places and causing offensive odours or additional problems with blow flies.

Insects

Insect infestations can be divided into those caused by flying insects, crawling insects and stored product insects.

Flying insects

There are many thousand of different types of fly, four of which are of concern as they lay their eggs in food. They are the housefly (*Musca domestica*), bluebottles (*Calliphora spp*), greenbottles (*Lucilia spp*) and the fruit fly (*Drosophila spp*).

Flies, with the exception of fruit flies, contaminate food in several ways:

◆ As they have no jaws, they feed by regurgitating enzymes (and usually part of the previous meal) onto food, trampling the enzymes into the food to soften it, then sucking the part-digested material through their proboscis. Flies do not discriminate between a meal on a rubbish tip or in your kitchen.
◆ All flies defecate as they eat.
◆ They carry bacteria on the hairs on their legs and bodies.
◆ They lay eggs in our food, the maggots eat and pupate in our food and the adults may die in our food.

The life cycle of these flies is temperature dependent and it may take as little as two weeks from egg to adult in warm weather. The hazards associated with houseflies, blue and green bottles are sometimes underestimated but these insects have been implicated in the transmission of many foodborne pathogens.

Fruit flies are more commonly found in bakeries, fruit factories and beer cellars. They prefer sweet liquid foods such as syrups and wine. They carry spoilage bacteria on their bodies but are perhaps less of a health hazard than the other species identified here.

Wasps

The wasp is particularly attracted to human foods during the late summer and early autumn. It favours sweet things, particularly over-ripe fruits. As they have jaws, their eating habits cause less contamination then those of flies. However, they can pick up pathogens as they crawl over rubbish. One of the main hazards associated with wasps is the panic they can cause amongst food handlers working in a busy kitchen.

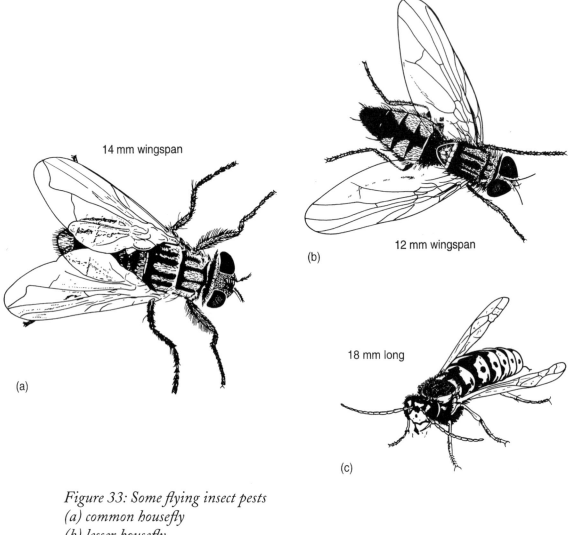

14 mm wingspan

12 mm wingspan

(b)

18 mm long

(c)

(a)

Figure 33: Some flying insect pests
(a) common housefly
(b) lesser housefly
(c) wasp

Control of flying insects

As with all food pests, the best method of control is to prevent access. This can be achieved through the use of screens on windows which open, and through the use of self-closing doors, plastic curtains or air doors. Good housekeeping and the hygienic disposal of waste will reduce the attraction of a food business to insects. The provision of electronic fly killers is the most effective method of killing flies in a kitchen. Sprays, vaporisers or impregnated strips should not be used in food environments.

Crawling insects

There are three types of crawling insects important as food pests. They are ants, cockroaches and silverfish.

Ants

Two types of ant may infest food, the black ant (garden ant) and Pharaoh's ants. Black ants are essentially garden insects which may become a serious nuisance if, as they forage, they enter a kitchen. They prefer sweet foods and may be controlled by the use of baited sugar syrups. Successful control depends upon the destruction of the nest.

Pharaoh's ants are pale yellow in colour and about 2mm in length. They need a constantly warm temperature and thus tend to be found in heated buildings. Like black ants, they prefer sweet foods but Pharaoh's ants will also seek out high protein foods such as meats. Again, successful control depends upon destruction of the nests, which may be very difficult to detect.

Cockroaches

There are two types of cockroach found in this country, the oriental cockroach (*Blatta orientalis*) and the German cockroach (*Blattella germanica*). The much larger American cockroach (*Periplaneta americana*) causes occasional problems when it escapes from laboratories, schools etc.

The oriental cockroach is by far the most common of the two species. It is about 25mm in length, brown in colour, has a flattish body and small vestigial wings. It cannot fly but can crawl through extremely small cracks and crevices. They are often found in damp places as they require water. The oriental cockroach lays its eggs in a case or ootheca which is attached to a solid surface. The insects hatch as minute replicas of the adults and shed their skins many times before reaching full size.

The German cockroach is less common. It is smaller than the oriental and is about 15mm in length. It has a flattish body and is a pale yellowish brown colour. It can climb smooth vertical surfaces such as painted walls. They prefer warm humid conditions and are often found in kitchens or restaurants. Both types of cockroach are nocturnal insects which feed off waste food. Their presence is usually detected by the identification of faecal pellets or the characteristic odour produced by the insects. Cockroaches carry pathogens including salmonella and *Staphylococcus aureus* although there is limited evidence that they commonly transfer these organisms to food.

Cockroach control

Cockroaches are particularly difficult to eradicate from food premises so preventing infestation is of primary importance. It is therefore important that all cracks, crevices and the points where pipes enter building are sealed. All incoming foodstuffs should be checked for signs of infestation as should non-food items such as laundry or furniture.

Effective control will require night time inspection to assess the extent of the infestation and the controlled use of an insecticide.

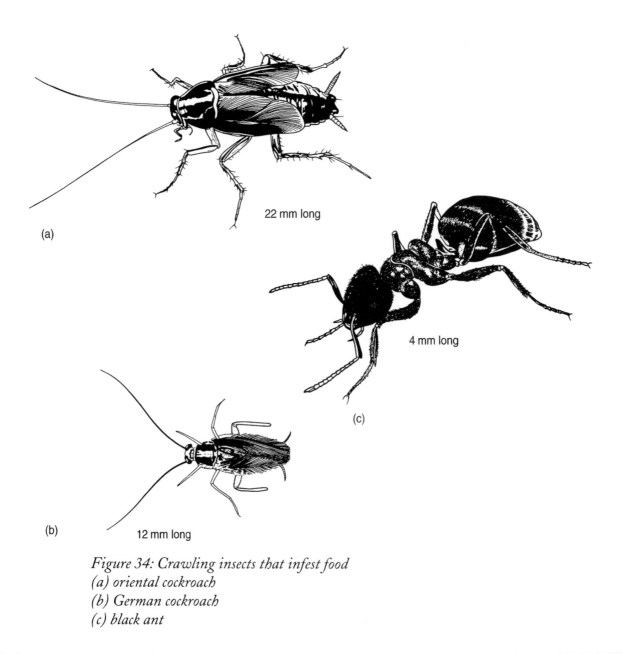

(a)

22 mm long

(c)

4 mm long

(b)

12 mm long

Figure 34: Crawling insects that infest food
(a) oriental cockroach
(b) German cockroach
(c) black ant

Silverfish

Silverfish are insects with 'fish-shaped' bodies and extremely long antennae. They live in damp environments and may be found under wallpaper or carpets. They are nocturnal and although they are unlikely to contaminate food directly, their presence should not be tolerated. Silverfish can be treated with contact insecticides.

Stored product insects

This title defines a large group of insects (beetles, weevils, moths and their larvae) which contaminate dried foodstuffs such as cereal grains, pastas, nuts, dried beans etc. Stored product insects have little or no direct implications for health but their presence in foods is undesirable for several reasons:

◆ insects breeding within a flour container could contaminate it with eggs, larvae, pupae and live or dead adults
◆ some stored product insects damage the quality of the food product; e.g. flour beetles reduce the gluten content of flour so that it makes poor quality baked products

Psocids (Book lice) are common stored product insects. They are 1–2mm in length and are difficult to see unless they move. They are also difficult to eliminate and extremely high standards of hygiene plus the use of residual insecticides is necessary.

Control of stored product insects

The successful control of this varied group of insects requires specific identification of the insects involved and the identification of the source, location and size of the infestation. Thorough control can only be successfully applied by a trained pest control operator, but it is likely to require the destruction of any suspect food.

Bird pests

Any bird which gains access to a food premises is classed as a pest. Most often the birds involved are feral pigeons and sparrows, although nesting swallows, blackbirds, seagulls and many other birds also cause problems. As with other potential pests, prevention is better than control. Consideration should be given during the planning and design of buildings to the potential ingress by birds. This should include the design of any new building without ledges or possible nesting or roosting sites. Like other pests, birds are attracted to buildings by the presence of food and so good housekeeping is essential.

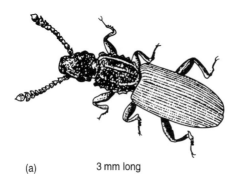

(a)　　　3 mm long

2.7 mm long

(d)

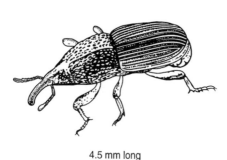

4.5 mm long

(b)

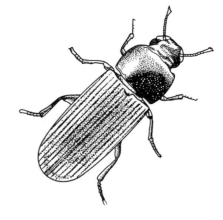

3.5 mm long

(e)

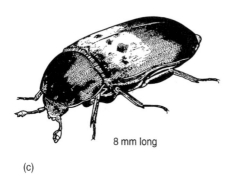

8 mm long

(c)

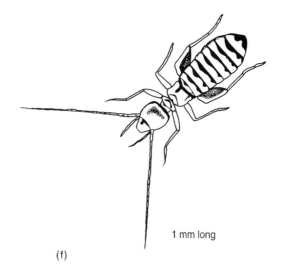

1 mm long

(f)

Figure 35: Stored product insects
(a) Saw-toothed grain beetle
(b) Grain weevil
(c) Larder beetle
(d) Biscuit beetle
(e) Confused flour beetle
(f) Psocid (Liposcelis bostrychophilus)

Control of bird pests

Inappropriate building design will attract birds and it may be extremely expensive to overcome any problems caused by poor design. Proofing a building against ingress by bird species is difficult, and the killing of many birds is prohibited under the Wildlife and Countryside Act 1981. This Act does make provision for the issue of a licence for the destruction of pest birds, but this is costly and frequently ineffective.

Why do we need to control food pests?

There are several reasons why it is necessary to control food pests:

◆ to prevent the spread of disease: as you have seen, all the main groups of food pests spread pathogenic or spoilage organisms and are therefore potential vectors of disease (or spoilage)
◆ to prevent food waste: infestation of food by stored product insects, the contamination of food by droppings, fur or feathers incur considerable costs to the food industry
◆ to comply with the law: The Food Safety Act 1990 makes it an offence to sell food contaminated with foreign bodies, or unfit food. Food contaminated in the ways described above could fall into this category
◆ to prevent damage to the premises: rodents gnaw to wear down their teeth which grow continuously during their lives. They will gnaw on anything, such as woodwork, metal pipes and electric cables. There have been instances where rodents have caused considerable damage and even fires by chewing through electric cables

General principles in controlling food pests

The animals, birds and insects identified in this section become food pests because they seek warmth, shelter, food, and peace and quiet to raise their young. To reduce the likelihood of a pest infestation the following general principles should be followed:

1 Design new buildings to prevent access to pests.

2 Maintain and proof old buildings thoroughly.

3 Inspect all buildings both inside and out on a regular basis for any signs of infestation of any sort.

4 Train all staff to look for and report possible signs of infestation.

5 Observe the principles of good housekeeping:

- ◆ keep the premises clean and tidy
- ◆ clear spillages away immediately
- ◆ rotate stock
- ◆ clean under and behind equipment regularly
- ◆ do not keep unwanted equipment or furniture
- ◆ maintain the area around the building to prevent the overgrowth of vegetation
- ◆ check all incoming items for signs of infestation.

EXERCISE

As you have read, the common food industry pests include rodents, insects, birds and rarely, other domestic or feral animals. It is particularly important that you are aware of the likely visible signs of pest infestation and understand the basic methods of control. In order to facilitate this you should prepare the following charts which will provide a summary of the material you have read and a useful 'at a glance' guide to the likely signs of pest infestation.

1   Either draw up a table which includes all the different groups of pests (rodents, insects, birds etc.) or draw up separate charts for each pest group.

2   Use the following column headings for each pest species:

- ◆ main identifying characteristics
- ◆ places to look for signs of infestation
- ◆ common signs of infestation
- ◆ other signs of infestation
- ◆ action.

SELF CHECK QUESTIONS

I   *List the main signs of rodent infestation.*

2   *What would you expect to find in the kitchen if there was a cockroach infestation?*

3   *What general rules would you give your staff concerning pest control?*

CLEANING AND DISINFECTING THE KITCHEN

By the end of this section you should be able to
- explain the difference between cleaning and disinfection
- list the components of an effective cleaning schedule
- identify those surfaces which require disinfection

The final section of this chapter examines the role of cleaning and disinfection in maintaining an hygienic and pest-free working environment. Cleaning and disinfection are essential processes in all catering operations. They are distinct processes which are equally important and should not be confused or combined. The efficiency with which the operations are performed affect the quality of the product being produced within the environment. Thinking about how to maintain high standards of hygiene and how cleaning and disinfection will be achieved begins at the planning stage of an operation. The use of chemicals in cleaning and disinfection is controlled by the Control of Substances Hazardous to Health Regulations 1994 (COSHH). These Regulations require employers to make available to employees information concerning the safe use of chemicals and all necessary safety equipment. Further information concerning the implications of the COSHH Regulations can be found in Chapter 5, page 84.

EXERCISE

Before you read this section there are several words which you need to understand accurately and in context. They are: **cleaning, disinfection, sterilisation, detergent, bactericidal, bacteriostatic**. Using your own words write a definition for each of the words listed. Check your definitions against those in the glossary at the back of this book.

What is cleaning?

Cleaning consists of three basic steps which can be summarised as follows:

◆ the removal of the visible dirt
◆ the removal of residual dirt using energy (physical, chemical or thermal)
◆ rinsing to remove residual dirt and any chemicals.

These steps may be followed by a disinfection procedure.

Cleaning should be performed at regular intervals but the actual methods which are used depend upon the nature of the dirt, the type of surface to be cleaned, the degree of water hardness and the standard of cleanliness required.

How cleaning is achieved

Cleaning requires the application of energy to effect the removal of dirt from a surface. Central to this definition is the use of energy. Energy can be input into the cleaning process in several ways:

Physical energy

Manual labour or machines often account for the greatest proportion of the cost of cleaning. The efficiency of labour depends upon the provision of suitable equipment, time and training.

Machines are available to perform many cleaning tasks and range from simple high pressure water hoses used to clean large food factories, to rotary floor scrubbers which can be used to clean and polish sealed floors, and domestic style vacuum cleaners. All cleaning machines are designed to meet certain needs and their planned use can reduce labour costs by increasing efficiency.

Thermal energy (hot water or steam)

As all chemical reactions occur more rapidly at higher temperatures, cleaning chemicals applied at higher temperatures will act more rapidly. However, at very high temperatures, safety problems can arise. For example, the use of steam as a cleaning agent must be carefully controlled as it is potentially very dangerous and can damage surfaces and equipment. The application of cleaning agents at very high temperatures may also damage surfaces and can cause noxious fumes to be generated. For these reasons cleaning chemical should **only** be used as directed by the manufacturer.

Chemical energy

Detergents are made from mixtures of soap-based chemicals which increase the wetting power of water to enable the removal of grease from surfaces. As with all chemicals, great care should be taken when handling detergents. Many of the commercially available products are not as 'user friendly' as the washing-up liquid you have at home.

Selecting a detergent

When selecting a detergent for use in a catering operation, it should be:

◆ readily soluble in water at the required temperature
◆ non-corrosive to surfaces, non-irritant to skin and non-toxic

◆ odourless
◆ biodegradable: in the past, problems have been caused in effluent disposal by the release of detergent into the system which then foamed and created environmental problems. The use of detergents which are degraded by effluent bacteria has overcome this problem
◆ economical for the use to which they are being put
◆ stable during storage
◆ active against a wide range of different types of dirt as this minimises the need for wide range of detergents within an operation.

Most detergents are carefully balanced 'cocktails' of chemicals selected to give the desired range of properties. Cost is an important consideration in the formulation of a detergent and thus the concentrations at which the agents are used are usually designed to maximise effect as economically as possible. Detergents may be available as powders or liquids. The former have the advantage of being more concentrated whilst the latter are perhaps easier to mix and dilute accurately.

Factors affecting the effectiveness of detergents

The most important factor which affects the use of detergents is that of the hardness of water. In addition, factors such as the concentration and the temperature of the solution also effect the efficacy of the agent, as does the **contact time** and the force with which it is applied.

In most cases these energy types are used in combination. Manual energy is the most expensive whilst chemical energy is the cheapest. Cost-effective cleaning depends upon the choice of the correct chemical for the appropriate task, applying it at the correct temperature in the correct concentration, and allowing it time to function.

Cleaning is a job for everyone

The standards of hygiene required in a catering operation must be clearly defined by management. The standards set should be practical and enforceable. Everyone working within the catering operation has a duty to ensure that satisfactory standards are maintained. Cleaning staff must be employed in sufficient numbers and must be trained for the tasks they perform. All other employees should be trained to clean-as-you-go, to maximise the efficiency of cleaning. Management must provide appropriate tools for the job and chemicals where appropriate. Cleaning schedules are usually used as a straightforward way of communicating information about procedures and standards. They also ensure that equipment, surfaces and premises are cleaned as required and using the correct agent. Such a written schedule should incorporate the following information:

◆ what is to be cleaned
◆ who is to clean it
◆ when it is to be cleaned
◆ how it is to be cleaned
◆ the chemicals and other materials, including safety equipment required
◆ appropriate precautions to be taken and protective clothing to be worn.

Additional considerations to be taken into account include the requirements of the Health and Safety at Work Act 1974, and the regulations concerning the Control of Substances Hazardous to Health Regulations (COSHH) 1994.

Problems caused by ineffective cleaning

A failure to clean a kitchen adequately will lead to the accumulation of food debris which may in turn lead to:

◆ a poor quality final product with a consequent reduction in its shelf-life
◆ customer complaints
◆ loss of reputation
◆ court proceedings
◆ food poisoning
◆ loss of sales
◆ food wastage.

Disinfection

When disinfecting food premises, it is rarely necessary to achieve sterility. The more common aim is to reduce the numbers of remaining bacteria to a level that will not affect the quality of the food products which come into contact with the surface/equipment etc.

Heat or chemicals can be used for the disinfection process, but must be preceded by thorough cleaning in each case. The activity of chemical disinfectants is impaired by the presence of dirt and therefore the cleaner the surface, the more effective the disinfection process will be.

Types of disinfection

Heat Disinfection

The application of heat, particularly wet heat such as steam, is the most reliable and effective means of destroying micro-organisms.
(**NB** think back to the effect of heat in food preservation, Chapter 7, page 108.)

Steam Disinfection

This system is used, particularly in factories, to clean equipment that is a difficult to reach. Steam cleaned equipment is self-drying but the use of steam may have adverse effects on certain pieces of equipment, e.g. certain plastics, paint may be removed by steam cleaning; it may remove lubricating grease from surfaces etc.

Chemical Disinfection

The types of chemical disinfectant for use in the catering industry are limited to those which are not likely to taint the food with unpleasant or toxic tastes or odours.

Selecting a disinfectant for use in a kitchen

When selecting a disinfectant for use in a kitchen the following factors should be considered:

1   The disinfectant should be capable of rapidly killing micro-organisms and equally effective against Gram positive and Gram negative organisms. (see page 182 for definitions)

2   The majority of mould spores should be killed; the destruction of a large proportion of bacterial spores would be an advantage.

3   It should be stable in the presence of organic residues and if necessary, depending on the geographical region, effective in the presence of hard water salts.

4   **Contact time:** this is the time that the disinfectant needs to be in contact with the item being disinfected to act effectively. It is important that all disinfectants are given adequate time to act, otherwise their use is a waste of time. Ideally the contact time should be such that the disinfectant can be wiped onto the surface and left so that it has a long period of activity and does not need to be removed from the surface.

5   In addition, the disinfectant should be:

<u>a</u>   non-corrosive and non-staining to the surface to which it is applied

<u>b</u>   odourless

<u>c</u>   non-toxic and non-irritant to personnel

d readily soluble in water and readily rinsing

e stable during prolonged storage in the concentrated form. Stability in the diluted form is an advantage but is usually only achieved in the short term.

f competitively priced and cost-effective in use.

Gram positive and Gram negative bacteria

The vast majority of bacteria are either Gram positive or Gram negative. This distinction is based upon the results of a staining technique developed by Johann Gram. The stain highlights differences in the structure of the bacterial cell wall. These differences affect the permeability of the cell wall to chemicals such as disinfectants and antibiotics. This is one of the main reasons why not all disinfectants (or antibiotics) are equally effective against all types of bacteria. It also explains why it is essential that disinfection selection is made by trained personnel.

The inactivation of disinfectants

Whilst there are many brands of disinfectant, they fall into relatively few chemical groups. Each brand in a particular group varies only slightly in its spectrum of activity. The variables that affect the activity of disinfectants include:

1 **Number of bacteria** A few bacteria may be killed easily whilst a larger population may be more difficult to kill. No disinfectant can be relied upon to kill all the bacteria present, but a kill of 99.9% is usually acceptable.

2 **Accessibility of the bacteria** To kill a bacteria, a disinfectant must touch a bacterial cell. Little is therefore achieved by pouring disinfectant over a surface which is dirty as the dirt will protect the bacteria present, particularly if the surface is also greasy. Hence the importance of a cleaning step which is effective before the application of the disinfectant.

3 **Temperature** The higher the temperature, the greater the activity of the disinfectant.

4 **Concentration** Unless used at the recommended concentration (or above), there is little point in using a disinfectant. The advantages of higher concentrations may be outweighed by the problems associated with skin irritation etc. and also the costs of using the agent too quickly.

5   **Volume**   A greater volume is more likely to be effective than a small volume because the effects of inactivation are reduced.

6   **pH**   Some disinfectants are sensitive to pH and in some types activity is better in alkaline conditions, while others work best in acid conditions.

7   **Time**   Disinfection is not instant: all disinfectants require time, measured as the **contact time** in which to act. Contact time depends upon the group into which the disinfectant falls, the concentration, the pH, the temperature. Gram negative bacteria die more slowly than gram positives under the same conditions.

8   **Inactivation**   All chemical disinfectants are inactivated by certain materials such as detergents, organic materials, hard water, plastics, cotton mop heads, cloths etc., nylon, and PVC.

Choice of disinfectant

Although there are hundreds of different brands of disinfectant currently available, they fall into a relatively small number of chemical groups. Few of these are suitable for use on food surfaces and even fewer have the beneficial properties described above. The disinfectants used in the food industry generally fall into the following five groups:

◆ Chlorine release agents
◆ Quaternary ammonium compounds
◆ Iodophors
◆ Amphoteric compounds
◆ Biguinides.

Table 18 on page 184 gives examples of some domestic brands of disinfectants which fall into the various chemical groups, together with some useful information about the properties of the disinfectants in the particular group.

The final choice of disinfectant will be based upon the sort of information given in the above table together with the following factors:

◆ the amount of dirt and debris
◆ the type of surface
◆ the possibility of taint
◆ the toxicity of the agent to be used and the possible effect on personnel (don't forget the COSHH implications)
◆ the method of disinfection to be used
◆ the contact time available
◆ the type of organisms to be destroyed.

Chemical Group	Properties	Domestic Brand
Chlorine compounds (Hypochlorites)	Broad spectrum of activity Some activity against bacterial spores Inactivated by hard water and organic materials e.g. food	Household bleaches
Phenolics	More active against Gram positive (e.g. S. aureus) than Gram negative (e.g. Salmonella) bacteria Inactive against bacterial spores Seriously inactivated by hard water, and organics materials, and moderately by man-made materials such as nylon and PVC	Dettol
QACs & Diguanides	Broad range of antibacterial activity although no activity against bacterial spores Seriously inactivated by hard water, organic and man-made materials	Savlon
Pine Fluids	Only have slight antibacterial activity and are not active against bacterial spores Seriously inactivated by hard water, organic materials and man-made materials	Pine fluids often retailed as 'own label' products in supermarkets

Table 18: The chemical groups and properties of some domestic disinfectants

Where to disinfect

It is not appropriate to disinfect all surfaces and pieces of equipment in a kitchen. For example, there is little point disinfecting the kitchen floor routinely as it will become dirty and contaminated almost immediately, but a preparation surface should be disinfected at regular intervals as part of the cleaning routine.

As a general rule the surfaces which should be disinfected regularly are those where the presence of micro-organisms at the levels usually found is unacceptable and could have an adverse effect on food quality or safety. In the catering environment these surfaces may include:

◆ food contact surfaces
◆ hand contact surfaces
◆ cleaning materials and equipment.

EXERCISE

You have already spent time in the kitchen observing people at work in the kitchen. However, the hygienic production of food does not stop once the food is ready to serve. The final part of the production cycle is the thorough cleaning of the kitchen, so for this exercise you will be examining the cleaning and disinfection procedures adopted in the kitchen.

1   Different aspects of cleaning and disinfection take place at points throughout the food production cycle. Ensure that you are familiar with all the different aspects of an effective cleaning regime.

2   You will need to know:

◆ What the COSHH Regulations state with regard to the storage and use of cleaning agents and disinfectants.
◆ What the COSHH Regulations state with regard to the use of cleaning agents and disinfectants.
◆ How and where the different chemicals should be used.
◆ What safety precautions should be taken when using the chemicals.
◆ What information you would expect on a cleaning schedule for the different areas/pieces of equipment in the kitchen.

3   Get a copy of the cleaning schedule for the kitchen you are investigating. Does it give all the information necessary for it to work effectively?

4   Observe as many different aspects of the cleaning and disinfection process as you can. Record your observations carefully. How does the implementation of the procedures compare with the schedules you have studied?

SELF CHECK QUESTIONS

1   *Define the following terms: cleaning, disinfection, bactericidal.*
2   *Why is it important to clean a surface thoroughly before it is disinfected?*
3   *Why is it inappropriate to make up a solution of a disinfectant, use it and then keep it until tomorrow?*

11

Managing Food Hygiene

The hygiene section of this book has introduced you to the many different aspects of food hygiene and to some basic food microbiology. All of this information needs to be applied as a matter of routine in a working catering operation. The best way to do this is the topic for this final chapter. Managing food hygiene is as important as managing the accounts, in fact it will impact directly upon the profitability of the business. Your role in this is crucial whatever your job, so it is important that you understand the basic principles involved in developing an integrated hygiene management strategy for a catering operation.

Why manage hygiene?

There are two main reasons why hygiene must be managed in a catering premises:

1　You have a legal responsibility to maintain adequate standards of food hygiene and to ensure that the food you prepare and sell is fit for consumption.

2　You have a moral responsibility to the well being of your customers.

There is evidence that the state of cleanliness and the operating practices in a food business directly affect the likelihood of food poisoning occurring. Studies have shown that the factors most frequently identified as being directly responsible for outbreaks of food poisoning remain the same, despite an increasing awareness of food safety issues.

For all types of food poisoning recorded the 'top ten' most frequently identified factors are:

◆ food prepared too far in advance of need
◆ food stored at room temperature (not kept cold or hot)
◆ food cooled too slowly before refrigeration
◆ food not re-heated properly
◆ using cooked food contaminated with food poisoning organisms
◆ under cooking food, particularly meat and meat products

◆ using contaminated canned food
◆ inadequate thawing
◆ cross-contamination
◆ raw food consumed.

NB   many outbreaks of food poisoning occur because of a combination of these factors.

Other factors identified include the contamination of food by infected food handlers and the use of leftovers. These findings have not changed from surveys conducted over a decade ago. All the factors reflect a failure to manage hygiene safely in the kitchen.

Until recently, hygiene management in catering operations has relied on reacting to problems when they were identified. This may be one reason why there has been little or no change in the factors listed above. Any attempt to manage hygiene has relied on an examination of problems in four main areas: people, premises, practices and plant (equipment) – the '4Ps', with limited consideration of the implications of any overlaps. In addition, action has usually only been taken once a problem has been identified, by which time it can only be corrective. Recent changes in food legislation have meant that there has been a move away from this traditional approach to managing hygiene in catering operations. The implementation of the Food Safety Act 1990, in particular the so called 'due diligence' defence, and the more recent Food Safety (General Food Hygiene) Regulations 1995 have lead to the implementation of a proactive approach to hygiene management. This involves managing the food production operation (regardless of size or method of operation) so that the potential hazards are identified, the risks of the hazards occurring are considered, and systems for managing them are developed.

Two such methods are considered in some detail in the remainder of this chapter. The first, the **Hazard Analysis Critical Control Point (HACCP)** technique was developed by the food industry where it is most widely used. The second, **Assured Safe Catering (ASC)** is a more recent development which is based upon the principles of HACCP. ASC has been specifically developed for the catering industry by the Department of Health because it was recognised that some catering operations would not have the resources or expertise to implement HACCP.

An introduction to HACCP

By the end of this section you should be able to
- define the acronym HACCP
- describe the basic steps necessary to set up an HACCP system

The Hazard Analysis Critical Control Point (HACCP – pronounced 'Hassop') approach to managing and controlling hazards was developed in the early 1960s. The original system was developed from ideas used in the engineering industry which were first applied to control the safety of food for astronauts during the space race. The HACCP approach applies a 'zero-defects' approach to the production of food, i.e. the idea that it is possible to produce a perfect (safe) product. In order to establish a HACCP system for a particular product (or closely related group of products), it is necessary to complete a detailed analysis of the hazards associated with:

- the food product
- the production process
- the equipment used to produce the product
- the production environment
- the production personnel, for each stage in the production process.

The risks of the hazards occurring at each stage are then considered and **critical control points (CCPs)** identified. A **critical control point (CCP)** is defined as *a point or procedure in a food production system where control can be exercised and the hazard eliminated or the probability of it occurring minimised.*

Once the CCPs have been identified, appropriate control systems, which can be monitored are put in place. These systems ensure that the limits by which the particular CCP is governed are not exceeded. If they are, immediate action is taken to remedy the situation. For example, a CCP requires that a cooking process heats a food product to 72°C ± 2°C and holds it at that temperature for two minutes. Should the temperature fail to reach 70°C, the CCP will not control the hazard. In this case it would be likely that a record would be made that the product failed to reach the appropriate temperature and so the heat treatment would be repeated.

Once all the CCPs have been identified for the particular production process, and all the appropriate control mechanisms are in place, the system manages food safety through control at selected CCPs. The development of supporting documentation is essential for the operation of a HACCP system. This documentation, which accompanies the product throughout the production process, is designed to detail all the controls and to record the measurements taken to assure the integrity of the CCPs. Using this documentation, it is then a very straightforward process to identify points where problems occur and to resolve them immediately.

It is beyond the scope of this text to provide the detailed information necessary to complete a hazard analysis; this chapter merely gives an overview of the main features of the system. HACCP was developed by the food manufacturing and processing industries to meet the specific needs of that type of operation. It is usually implemented by a multi-disciplinary team of individuals, each with specialised knowledge of different aspects of the food production process. For this reason its transfer to catering has been limited to large systematic catering operations which using modern technologies, such as cook chill and sous-vide.

Whilst it can be cumbersome, the HACCP system can provide useful evidence of 'due diligence', should legal problems arise concerning a food item produced. Partly for this reason, and because the EU Hygiene Directive requires food businesses to use HACCP principles when developing hygiene management systems, the Department of Health has launched a modified system for use in catering operations. This system is called Assured Safe Catering (ASC) and the remainder of this chapter examines it in detail and considers how you can make it work in your operation.

SELF CHECK QUESTION

What does the acronym HACCP stand for?

ASSURED SAFE CATERING

By the end of this section you should be able to
- describe how the ASC system operates
- list the steps necessary to implement ASC in a catering operation

The Department of Health set up the Assured Safe Catering group to develop a modified HACCP system for caterers that was more 'user friendly'. Like HACCP, the ASC approach to managing food hygiene and safety enables you to prevent problems occurring by identifying hazards associated with each step in your operation. Once you have identified the possible hazards, it is necessary to identify the appropriate critical control points (CCPs) which can be used to prevent the hazards occurring. It is a systematic process which can be readily implemented if you follow the basic steps outlined below.

Before you start there are some definitions that need to be understood:

1   **Hazard**   A hazard is something that has the potential to cause harm to the consumer. Three groups of hazards are identified:

   a̲   **Biological**: these may be micro-organisms or pests

   b̲   **Physical**: e.g. glass, plastic or metal

   c̲   **Chemical:** e.g. pesticides, disinfectants.

2   **Risk**   A risk is the likelihood that the hazard will occur.

3   **Critical control point (CCP)**   A CCP is the step in the process which must be controlled to ensure that the hazard(s) identified are either eliminated or reduced to a level which is safe.

Setting up an ASC system

There are seven basic steps in the ASC procedure.

Step 1   Planning

Whatever the scale of your operation, some planning is essential so that normal working routines are not disrupted. An ASC system should be introduced gradually to allow for changes to be made in the workplace. The successful implementation of ASC requires the full co-operation of your workforce, so you should allow time for employees to become used to new procedures.

Step 2   The Assured Safe Catering team

If possible, the implementation of ASC should be undertaken by a team of people working towards a common goal. It is unlikely that one individual will have all the necessary expertise to be able to identify all the likely hazards and appropriate control mechanisms.

It is possible for one person to develop an ASC system, but remember two (or more) heads are better than one.

Step 3   Draw a flow chart

Whether the kitchen you work in operates a traditional cook-serve system or a large scale cook chill system, ASC can provide a logical hygiene management system. Broadly speaking, all catering operations operate to the same basic series of process steps. These are shown in Figure 36. Using this flow chart you should be able to trace the series of process steps used to produce food in the operation in which you work.

Step 4   Hazard Analysis

Step 4 is divided into the six stages of a HACCP analysis:

<u>a</u>   list hazards

<u>b</u>   identify controls

<u>c</u>   critical control points

<u>d</u>   a recording system

<u>e</u>   implement

<u>f</u>   monitor

For each stage in the flow chart you have drawn, it is necessary to go through steps a–f, rather like the original HACCP system. Remember, as far as possible you must identify ALL the hazards, biological, chemical and physical for each stage.

A hazard is anything which could cause harm to the consumer

You may find it helpful to ask yourself the following set of questions so that you don't forget anything:

1   **What does this stage do?**   For example, purchasing brings food into the operation, cooking heats food to a specific temperature for a specific time.

2   **Where do the likely contaminants come from?**   For example, for the receipt step, contaminants may come from the transport vehicles and its driver, from the containers in which food is delivered, from poor temperature control or from poor quality food.

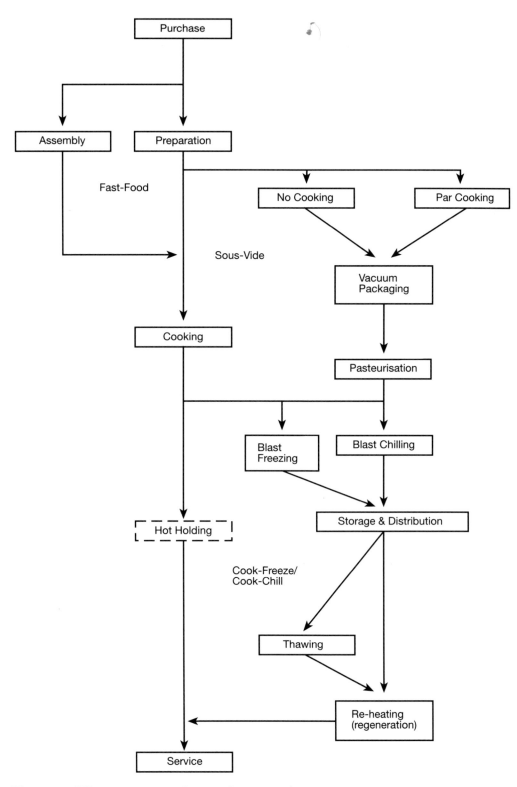

Figure 36: The process stages in catering operations

3   **What do I need to ensure about the food when it moves to the next stage in the process?**   For example, in the storage stage you would need to ensure that food was sent to the kitchen within its shelf-life, at the correct temperature and in an appropriate container. You would also need to ensure that the food was stored properly in the kitchen prior to use – it may be appropriate to include another storage step prior to preparation.

Having identified all the hazards, you can move on to identifying the control measures. Try to use controls that your business has the technology to implement properly, e.g. use those that rely on cooking times and temperatures to control the hazards rather than those which require more complex measurements.

Next, think carefully about which of the stages in the operation are CCPs. Table 19 shows some CCPs and the types of appropriate control actions. This is not a complete list of all CCPs and controls, rather it gives you some of the more common examples likely to be found in most operations.

Use the following questions to decide if a process stage is a CCP:

◆ Can the hazard be eliminated or reduced by this stage?
◆ Can the hazard be eliminated or reduced by a later process stage?
◆ Which of the process stages identified is most appropriate to control the hazard?

To answer this last question, think about how you will monitor the CCPs you have identified and perhaps equally importantly, **who** will monitor them.

Each of the CCPs you identify should have **critical limits** within which it must operate. These limits will depend upon the type of control and the type of monitoring you select. For example if you identify cooking as the main CCP, and time/temperature measurements as the monitoring process, you may select 75°C as the critical temperature with a tolerance of ±2°C so that a temperature measurement of between 73°C and 77°C would be acceptable.

Step 5   Repeat stage 4 for each stage in your operation

Once you have completed step 4 repeat the whole process until ASC is operating at each stage in your operation. Don't worry if it seems to take a long time to get through all the stages, it is better to implement the system slowly and thoroughly than to rush and end up with a system that doesn't work.

Step	Hazard	Action
1 *Purchase*	High risk (ready to eat) foods contaminated with food poisoning bacteria or toxins.	Buy from reputable supplier only. Specify temperature at delivery.
2 *Receipt*	High risk (ready to eat) foods contaminated with food poisoning bacteria or toxins.	Visual/sensory checks. Temperature checks.
3 *Storage*	Growth of food poisoning bacteria, toxins on high risk (ready to eat) foods. Further contamination.	High risk foods stored at safe temperatures. Store wrapped. Date label high risk foods. Rotate stock and use by recommended date.
4 *Preparation*	Contamination of high risk (ready to eat) foods. Growth of pathogenic bacteria.	Limit exposure to ambient temperatures during preparation. Prepare with clean equipment used for high risk (ready to eat) foods only. Separate cooked and raw foods. Wash hands before handling food.
5 *Cooking*	Survival of pathogenic bacteria.	Cook rolled joints, chicken, and reformed meats e.g. burgers to at least 75°C in the thickest part. Sear the outside of other meats (e.g. joints of beef, steaks) before cooking.
6 *Cooling*	Growth of any surviving spores or pathogens. Toxin production. Contamination with pathogenic bacteria.	Cool foods as quickly as possible. Do not leave out at room temperatures to cool unless cooling period is short (e.g. place stews, rice etc. in shallow tray and cool to chill temperatures quickly).
7 *Hot holding*	Growth of pathogenic bacteria. Toxin production.	Keep food hot, e.g. above 63°C.
8 *Reheating*	Survival of pathogenic bacteria.	Reheat to above 75°C.
9 *Chilled storage*	Growth of pathogenic bacteria.	Temperature control. Date code high risk (ready to eat) foods. Use in rotation and always within shelf life.
10 *Service*	Growth of pathogens. Toxin production. Contamination.	*Cold service* – serve high risk foods as soon as possible after removing from refrigerated storage. *Hot foods* – serve high risk foods quickly.

Table 19: Critical control points in catering operations
Source: Assured Safe Catering: A Management System for Hazard Analysis,
HMSO. *Reproduced with permission from the Department of Health*

Step 6   Check the system

Once the full ASC system is operating you will need to review the situation to ensure that it is all operating as you intended: i.e. ensure that all the CCPs are being correctly implemented and monitored, and that all your staff are coping with the new system.

Step 7   A full review

Once the system has been operating for a while you should review procedures again and iron out any problems. Don't change things unless your original control is unworkable or inadequate. Modifications may be necessary at some point in time but they should not be undertaken unless they are really necessary. Whilst the whole idea of ASC is that it is a flexible and adaptable system, constant change will confuse your staff and will result in an unworkable system.

This step should be carried out periodically to review the whole ASC system for your operation. Remember that new staff must be trained and they should understand the reasons why they must monitor CCPs effectively.

Developing an ASC system for your business

If the various steps in the implementation and review of an ASC system are followed, the system will become very specialised for your business. It will operate to those procedures which work for you and your staff. Remember that implementing ASC is likely to require that you train staff. The Food Hygiene (General Food Safety) Regulations 1995 require that all food handlers are trained to a level appropriate to the tasks they will have to perform. This type of training is essential for the efficient operation of an ASC system, so it is a good idea to build an appropriate training programme into the development of an ASC system.

An effective ASC system will also provide evidence that your business is taking all reasonable precautions to prevent food contamination and food poisoning. The documentation associated with the system can provide evidence that your business is operating with all due diligence, under the terms of the Food Safety Act 1990 and therefore may act as a defence should you face legal action.

Implementing ASC is time consuming and may well incur costs to some operations. However, once in place the system should start to save you money by preventing problems arising, minimising the impact of those which do and helping to maintain your business reputation. It is a new approach to the management of hygiene, particularly for caterers, as it requires you to think of your operation much more systematically. To help you further with the implementation of ASC, the Department of Health has produced two booklets about ASC, which are listed in the Useful Publications List at the end of this book. Your local Environmental Health Officer can also provide advice and practical help on the development of an ASC system for your business.

EXERCISE

If you have completed the observation and practical exercises given in chapters 8–10 of this book, you will have had good practice at identifying hazards in the kitchen. You need to develop these hazard identification skills for ASC. Now return to the kitchen and repeat the observations for a specific food preparation process. Complete the ASC steps (particularly step 4) for each of the hazards you identify.

SELF CHECK QUESTIONS

1   *What does the acronym ASC stand for?*
2   *Define the terms hazard and critical control point assured in ASC.*
3   *What are the seven steps in the ASC process?*
4   *What benefits would an ASC system have for a catering operation?*

APPENDIX 1
Useful Publications

The Health of the Nation White Paper (1992) HMSO

Food Sense Leaflets. These are free publications available from Food Sense, London, SE99 7TT. Titles available:
> Food Safety
> Understanding Food Labels
> Understanding Food Additives
> Food Protection
> Healthy Eating
> The New Microwave Labels
> Food and Pesticides
> Monitoring our food and nutrition
> Natural toxicants in our food
> Food Emergencies

The National Food Survey, Ministry of Agriculture, Fisheries and Food; published by HMSO annually

Dietary Reference Values: A Guide, (1991) Department of Health HMSO

Nutritional Aspects of Cardiovascular Disease, (1994) Committee on Medical Aspects of Food Policy, Department of Health, HMSO

Eat well: An action plan for the Nutrition Task Force to achieve the Health of the Nation targets on diet and nutrition, (1994) Department of Health

Eight Guidelines for a Healthy Diet, (1990) Food Sense

Implementing Healthy Catering Practice, (1992) Technical Brief No. 11 HCIMA 191 Trinity Road, London, London, SW 17 7HN

Healthy Catering Practice, (1993) The Health of the Nation, Department of Health

Nutrition Guidelines for Hospital Catering, (1995) The Health of the Nation, Department of Health

A Template: Industry Guides to Good Hygiene Practice, (1995) BAPs Health Publication Unit, Storage & Distribution Centre, Heywood Stores, Manchester Road, Heywood, Lancs. OL10 2PZ

Food Safety (Temperature Control) Regulations, (1995), HMSO

Guidance on the Food Safety (Temperature Control) Regulations, (1995), Department of Health HMSO

Chilled and Frozen: Guidelines on Cookchill and Cookfreeze systems, (1989) Department of Health

Food Safety (General Food Hygiene) Regulations, (1995), HMSO

Food Safety Act, (1990), HMSO

Assured Safe Catering: A Management System for Hazard Analysis, (1993) Department of Health, HMSO

Howells, G., Bradgate, R., & Griffiths, M., (1990) *Blackstone's Guide to the Food Safety Act*, Blackstone Press Ltd, London

Hugill, J., (1986) *Report of the Committee of Inquiry into an Outbreak of Food Poisoning at Stanley Royd Hospital*, HMSO

Jukes, D.J., (1983) *Food Legislation of the UK: A Concise Guide*, 3rd Edn, Butterworth-Heinemann, Oxford

Holland, B. *et al* (1991) *McCance and Widdowson's The Composition of Foods*, 5th edn, Royal Society of Chemistry and Ministry of Agriculture, Fisheries and Food (and supplements)

O'Mahony, M. *et al* (1990) *An Outbreak of foodborne botulism associated with contaminated hazelnut yoghurt*, Epidemiology and Infection, 104, 389–395

APPENDIX 2
Dietary Reference Values

The Dietary Reference Values for energy protein, selected vitamins and minerals are on the table on page 202. Values for other nutrients are given below.

Fat

	% Energy (excluding alcohol)
Saturated fatty acids	11
Cis – monounsaturated fatty acids	13
Cis – polyunsaturated fatty acids	6.5
Total Fat	35

Carbohydrates (sugars and starches)

Starches, intrinsic sugars (sugars contained with cell walls of food) and lactose	39
Sucrose and other extrinsic sugars (e.g. honey)	11
Total Carbohydrate	50

(alcohol is excluded and protein is at current level of 15%)

Non-starch polysaccharides (fibre)

Non-starch polysaccharides 18g/day, range 12 to 24g/day. Children should eat less as they weigh less.

Notes

Dietary Reference Values are intended to apply to healthy people. They do not make any allowance for the difference energy and nutrient needs imposed by some diseases.

The term Dietary Reference Value is a general term used to cover all the figures produced by the authors of the Dietary Reference Values report (see Useful Publications list for full details).

Other useful terms include:

Estimated Average Requirement – estimate of the average requirement for food energy or a nutrient. Clearly many people will need more than the average and many people will need less.

Reference Nutrient Intake – an amount of a nutrient that is enough for almost every individual, even someone who has high needs for the nutrient. This level of intake is therefore considerably higher than most people need. If individuals are consuming the RNI of a nutrient they are most unlikely to be deficient in that nutrient.

DIETARY REFERENCE VALUES: SUMMARY
DEPARTMENT OF HEALTH 1991

Reference Nutrient Intake

Age Range	Estimated Average Requirements ENERGY kcal/day	PROTEIN g/day	VITAMIN A retinol equiv µg/day	THIAMIN mg/day	RIBOFLAVIN mg/day	NIACIN Nicotinic acid equivalent mg/day	VITAMIN C mg/day	VITAMIN D µg/day	CALCIUM mg/day	IRON mg/day	SODIUM mg/day
Boys <1	545–920	12.5–14.9	350	0.2–0.3	0.4	3–5	25	8.5 (0–6 m)	525	1.7–7.8	210–350
1–3	1230	14.5	400	0.5	0.6	8	30	7.0 (6 m–3 y)	350	6.9	500
4–6	1715	19.7	500	0.7	0.8	11	30	–	450	6.1	700
7–10	1970	28.3	500	0.7	1	12	30	–	550	8.7	1200
11–14	2220	42.1	600	0.9	1.2	15	35	–	1000	11.3	1600
15–18	2755	55.2	700	1.1	1.3	18	40	–	1000	11.3	1600
Men 19–50	2550	55.5	700	1.0	1.3	17	40	–	700	8.7	1600
Men 50+	2550	53.3	700	0.9	1.3	16	40	(65+ 10µg/day)	700	8.7	1600
Girls <1	515–865	12.5–14.9	350	0.2–0.3	0.4	3–5	25	8.5 (0–6 m)	525	1.7–7.8	210–350
1–3	1165	14.5	400	0.5	0.6	8	30	7.0 (6 m–3 y)	350	6.9	500
4–6	1545	19.7	500	0.7	0.8	11	30	–	450	6.1	700
7–10	1740	28.3	500	0.7	1	12	30	–	550	8.7	1200
11–14	1845	41.2	600	0.7	1.1	12	35	–	800	14.8	1600
15–18	2110	45.4	600	0.8	1.1	14	40	–	800	14.8	1600
Women 19–50	1940	45	600	0.8	1.1	13	40	–	700	14.8	1600
Women 50+	1900	46.5	600	0.8	1.1	12	40	(65+ 10µg/day)	700	8.7	1600

For further details see Dietary Reference Values A Guide DH, 1991, HMSO

APPENDIX 3
Relevant targets from the Health of the Nation White Paper

Coronary Heart Disease (CHD) and Stroke targets:

◆ to reduce death rates for both CHD and stroke in people under 65 by at least 40% by the year 2000 (Baseline 1990)

◆ to reduce the death rate for CHD in people aged 65 to 74 by at least 30% by the year 2000 (Baseline 1990)

◆ to reduce the death rate for stroke in people aged 65 to 74 by at least 40% by the year 2000 (Baseline 1990)

Dietary and nutrition targets:

◆ to reduce the average percentage of food energy derived by the population from fat to 35% by the year 2005

◆ to reduce the average percentage of food energy derived by the population from saturated fatty acids to 11% by the year 2005

◆ to reduce the proportion of men and women aged 16–64 who are obese by at least 25% and 33% respectively by 2005 (Baseline 1986/7)

◆ to reduce the proportion of men drinking more than 21 units of alcohol per week and women drinking more than 14 units per week by 30% by 2005. (There has been a recent change to this recommendation: men are now being advised to consume no more than 4 units per day, and women 3 units per day.)

Blood Pressure

◆ to reduce mean systolic blood pressure in the adult population by at least 5mm Hg by 2005

Glossary

Acidophilic—used to describe micro-organisms which thrive in acidic conditions.

Aflatoxins—a toxin originally identified in the mould _Aspergillus flavus_ from which these toxins get their name.

Amino acids—the units that make up proteins.

Amylose—a starch with the saccharide units in unbranched chains.

Amylopectin—the greater part of dietary starch with the saccharide units in branched chains.

Anaemia—low concentration of haemoglobin in the blood causing tiredness and other symptoms. Deficiencies of iron, folic acid and vitamin B_{12} result in different types of anaemia.

Aseptic—free from all micro-organisms.

Asexual—the term used to describe reproduction which does not involve the uniting of male and female.

Autotrophic nutrition—the use of chemically simple organic substances as food.

Bacterial colony—a group of bacterial cells on a surface, usually an agar plate, which arise from the division of a single 'mother' cell.

Bactericidal—chemicals which will destroy vegetative bacterial cells but not necessarily bacterial spores.

Bacteriostatic—chemicals which prevent the growth of bacteria.

Binary fission—the division of one cell into two.

Biodegradable—capable of being broken down by bacteria or other organisms.

Blanched—the rapid heating and then cooling of some fruits and vegetables used to destroy enzymes.

Body Mass Index (BMI)—used as an indicator of overweight or obesity. The weight in kilograms divided by the height in metres squared.

Broad spectrum of activity—used to describe disinfectants which are active against a wide range of micro-organisms.

Budding—the process of asexual reproduction observed in yeasts, whereby a bud develops on the surface of the 'mother' cell and eventually splits off to become a new independent cell.

Capsule—a layer of mucous which is present on the surface of some bacterial cells.

Carriers—an individual who carries, and may transmit, disease-causing bacteria without showing any apparent signs of illness.

Cis fatty acids—a form of unsaturated fatty acid in which the hydrogen atoms are arranged on one side of the double band. Naturally occurs in a range of fat and oil containing foods.

Cases—an individual who shows symptoms of food poisoning.

Cleaning—the process of removing dirt.

Conidia—the term used to describe the way in which the spores of moulds are arranged at the tip of the reproductive hyphae.

Contact time—the time a disinfectant or cleaning agent needs to be in contact with a surface for maximal effect.

Convalescent carriers—an individual who has suffered from food poisoning, recovered but who still carries the bacteria and could transmit it.

Critical control point (CCP)—a point or procedure in a food production system where control can be exercised and the hazard or the risks of it occurring minimised.

Cross contamination—the transfer of micro-organisms from one place to another.

Danger zone—the temperature range in which microbial growth is most rapid i.e. between 5°C–63°C.

Decline phase—the final stage in the bacterial growth curve. The numbers within the population dying exceed those forming.

Detergent—a chemical made of soap or synthetic substitutes which are used to remove grease and dirt in cleaning.

Dietary fibre—plant material in the diet that resists digestion by human gut enzymes. Also known as roughage. Non-starch polysaccharide is now the accepted term.

Dietary Reference Values—a general term to cover all the dietary standards used in the UK.

Disinfection—the destruction of micro-organisms, but not bacterial spores, to a level which is neither harmful to health or likely to lead to the reduction in the quality of perishable foods.

DNA—Deoxyribonucleic acid. The main constituent of the nucleus of all cells.

E numbers—a system of numbering food additives introduced by the European Union.

Essential amino acids—those amino acids that are essential in the diet.

Essential fatty acids—polyunsaturated fatty acids that are essential in the diet.

Facultative—able to grow under both aerobic and anaerobic conditions.

Faecal—present in faeces.

Faecal oral—the oral (i.e. by mouth) ingestion of micro-organisms present in faeces, either directly or indirectly.

Fatty acids—the major components of fats. Consist of chains of carbon atoms with hydrogen atoms and an acid group attached. If there are no double bonds in the chain – saturated fatty acid, one double bond – monounsaturated, two or more double bonds – polyunsaturated.

Fertile hypha—see hypha. A reproductive hypha found in moulds, will bear asexual spores.

Flagella—a long threadlike attachment found on some bacterial cells. Facilitates movement.

Food allergy—intolerance to a food that involves an abnormal immunological reaction.

Food intolerance—a reproducible unpleasant reaction to a food that is not psychologically based.

Food spoilage—The process which leads to food being damaged or injured such that it is unfit for human consumption.

Foreign bodies—any material not normally present in food.

Genera—the taxonomic grouping containing many species, for example the genus *Salmonella* contains over 2000 different species, such as *Salmonella typhi*, *Salmonella paratyphi*, *Salmonella enteritidis*, *Salmonella typhimurium*.

Generation time—the time it takes for one bacterial cell to become two, for two to become four etc.

Halophilic—used to describe organisms which thrive in high concentrations of NaCl (Salt).

Hazard analysis critical control point (HACCP)—a system of food safety management based upon the identification of all the potential hazards within a food production system, and their control at specific points (critical control points).

Healthy carrier—individual who carries a disease-causing bacteria but who does not show any symptoms of illness.

Heterotrophic nutrition—require chemically complex substances, such as proteins and carbohydrates, for food.

High risk food—food which readily supports microbial growth. Usually short shelf-life foods rich in protein, e.g. raw meat, raw fish, eggs, milk and dairy products.

Hypha—the filaments that make up the main body of a mould. When growing on food they appear as a furry mass. Some hyphae (plural) are specialised and bear reproductive spores, these are called reproductive hyphae.

Incidents—either an outbreak or sporadic case of food poisoning.

Inorganic—substances which do not have the structure of living organisms, do not contain carbon i.e. those which are not organic.

Joule—the Standard International Unit of energy. Kilojoule (kJ) = 1000 joules; Megajoule (MJ) = a million joules; 4.2kJ = 1kcal.

Kcal, kilocalories—commonly used in nutrition as the measure of the energy value of food, Calorie (with a capital C) and kcal are taken to mean the same thing.

Lag phase—the first stage in the bacterial growth curve. Growth results in an increase in cell size rather than an increase in cell numbers.

Lipids—term used to describe fats and oils.

Log phase—the second stage in the bacterial growth curve. The period of rapid growth which occurs by the continual doubling of the population.

Market diseases—those microbial diseases responsible for the spoilage of fruit and vegetable crops before they can be consumed.

Mesophilic—the term used to describe bacteria which grow best at temperatures in the region 15°C–45°C.

Microaerophilic—the term used to describe bacteria which grow best in the presence of small amounts of oxygen.

Mycotoxins—the general term used to describe all the different types of toxins produced by moulds.

Neutrophilic—the term used to describe micro-organisms which thrive at pHs around neutrality.

Non-starch polysaccharide (NSP)—dietary polysaccharides other than starch, cannot be digested by gut enzymes, they make up the bulk of dietary fibre.

Non-pathogenic—micro-organisms which do not cause disease.

Nucleic acid—DNA or RNA.

Nutrient dense foods—foods containing a range of nutrients in a small volume of food.

Obligate aerobes—organisms which can only grow in the presence of oxygen.

Obligate anaerobes—organisms which can only grow in the absence of oxygen.

Organic—substances which contain carbon, relating to living things.

Osmophilic—the term used to describe organisms which thrive at high osmotic pressures, for example in high sugar concentrations.

Outbreaks—two or more individuals infected with the same food poisoning organism and who can be related in place and time.

Parasite—an animal or plant that lives off another (the host), usually to its detriment.

Pasteurisation—the process of heating foods to such a temperature that all pathogenic micro-organisms, and most spoilage micro-organisms are destroyed.

Pathogenic—disease causing.

Permanent carriers—those individuals who have been infected with and continue to harbour pathogenic bacteria.

Permanent excretors—those individuals who have been infected with pathogenic bacteria and continue to excrete them in their faeces.

pH—a measure of the acidity or alkalinity of a substance. pH is measured on a scale of 0–14 where 0 is the most acid and 14 is the most alkali. A pH of 7 is neither acid nor alkali, it is neutral.

Photosynthesise—the means by which plants and some micro-organisms make food from sunlight, water and simple organic compounds.

Psychrophilic—the term used to describe organisms which thrive at low temperatures, usually in the range.

Rodenticide—a chemical used to destroy rodents.

RNA—ribonucleic acid. The nucleic acid involved in protein synthesis.

Saprophytes—an organism which lives off dead and decomposing organic material.

Soluble fibre/non-starch polysaccharide—that part of NSP that forms gums of gels when mixed with water. The insoluble fibre is insoluble in water and consists mainly of cellulose.

Spoilage organisms—those micro-organisms that are involved in food spoilage.

Sporadic incidents—single cases of food poisoning which do not appear to be related to any other in a given time period.

Sporangium—a term used to describe the 'container' in which spores are produced in some moulds.

Stationary phase—the third stage in the bacterial growth curve. The same number of cells are being produced as are dying, so there is no increase in the size of the population. Usually food is becoming scarce and the concentration of waste materials is increasing.

Sterilisation—the process of destroying all micro-organisms and their spores.

Substrate—a substance upon which an enzyme acts.

Thermophilic—the term used to describe organisms which thrive at high temperatures, usually 40°C–80°C.

Trans fatty acids—a form of unsaturated fatty acid in which the hydrogen atoms are arranged on opposite sides of the double bonds. Major sources are vegetable oils that have been hydrogenated, i.e. have had hydrogen added to them artificially.

Vegetarian—a person who eats only food of vegetable origin. The prefixes lacto- (milk), ovo- (eggs), and pesco- (fish) are used if these animal foods are eaten. A vegan avoids all animal foods.

Vegetative—the term used to describe cells which reproduce asexually.

Vehicle—the term used to describe something which can transfer bacteria from place to place. Some common vehicles are hands, cloths, knives, food contact surfaces.

Water activity—a measurement of the amount of water in a product that is available for microbial growth.

Index